How My Wife, My Legal Partner, was Stolen

From Me When I Was Not Looking

Due to Carmel Murray's Dementia, her relatives placed her in a Nursing Home without my Knowledge. These are some of the Many Actions I am Forced to Take to Bring Carmel back Home

By

Tom Richard

A Practical GUIDE and GUIDELINES to protect you no matter if you're Partners, Married, Gay or Straight - and what you can do to make sure this Horrible Situation Does NOT happen to You!

Dedication and Guidelines

This 'Guide' is dedicated to all of those suffering from the absence of a loved one – particularly those loved ones who have been STRIPPED from you illegally.

This guide is written for you. It provides practical professional Guidelines based on what I, Tom Richards, have gone through when my deal wife and Legal Parter was STOLEN from me by Carmel's relatives. Unfortunately, this happens all the time and is usually do to 'Money', Greed and selfishness. The book starts with a background of Carm and my loving relationship. A sort of 'history' that shows all who read this how much we love each other and why I want her home so desperately. That background is followed by chapters that provide relatively short anecdotes about the following Guidelines.

I very much hope that these help all who read this very short book.

Tom Richards, Author

(the Guidelines are MY RESPONSIBILITY and based on my personal experience. Do NOT take them at face value. Seek additional advice from a professional if you need it

Table of content

Dedication and Guidelines iv
Chapter One 7
Chapter Two: 15
Chapter Three 19
Chapter Four 29
Chapter Five 42
Guideline Number 3 55
Guideline Number 4 66
Guideline Number 5 83
Guideline Number 6 94
Guideline Number 7 102
Guideline Number 8 108
Guideline Number 9 121
Guideline Number 10 135
Guideline Number 11 140
Guideline Number 12 144
Appendix: 148
Acknowledgements 153

Guideline Number 1

1. <u>Keep asking important questions.</u> The Answer are often Confusing and Stupid Beyond Belief. And usually, those answering your questions are lying to you. Or, all you'll hear from them is SILENCE.

Guideline Number 2

2. <u>Understand the Relevant Laws in Your Country regarding Legal Guardianship, Next of Kin, Legal Decision Makers, Power of Attorney, Wills, and Various Healthcare Acts.</u> Prior to Carm's hospitalisation, we didn't and I very much regret it.

Guideline Number 3

3. <u>… you MUST do that. When you do, you can then help your loving spouse, partner or friend with any illness, problem or issue at all.</u>

Guideline Number 4

4. <u>In the US, you'll need a good lawyer.</u> In Europe, under the Torte system of Justice, you'll need a good solicitor and will also have to retain a Barrister at some point. If relevant to your situation, do that as soon as you can

Guideline Number 5

5. <u>… and by EXHAUSTIVE, I mean it!</u> – on Dementia, Alzheimer's and similar mental diseases. Lawyers, Barristers, Solicitors. Local and national Politicians. Influencers like

Psychiatrists and Directors of Nursing. Friends and relatives that can DEMONSTRATE the length of your relationship and how you loved each other. And this is just SOME of the research.

Guideline Number 6

6. <u>... ALL THE TIME!</u> Do your very best to get over that horrible reality. For years, I couldn't. For all sorts of reasons, it prevented me from taking ACTION.

Guideline Number 7

7. <u>Trying Your Very Best is all you can do.</u> In the past, when Carm was stolen, I beat myself up emotionally every day. I don't do that as often, now, but on some mornings I feel like someone is beating my head in with an axe.

Guideline Number 8

8. <u>Guilt is like Rust.</u> It eats you up and leaves only a husk of your former self. If you think you need help coping, go out and get it!

Guideline Number 9

9. <u>Keep Active & Enjoy Life</u>... With a Strong Focus on your Objectives, Discipline and a strong work ethic. Enjoying life with many activities will help you pass the time until you / I can see (insert name here) Carm my Missing Partner / Wife / Life

Guideline Number 10

10. <u>Keep Active and Enjoy Life!!!</u> We are Entitled to a Future of Happiness, Joy and contentment – don't forget your own needs. My good friends and family members all say that I need to get out there to do what Carm and I used to do together.

Guideline Number 11

11. <u>Learn to Share with Close Friends.</u> When you do, when you find those people who you can trust to share a secret or two, you'll feel much better.

Guideline Number 12

12. <u>Hope. A Profound Sometimes Gift.</u> Hope can be very elusive. But HOPE gives all of us strength to face the uncertainty that we all go through sometimes for a lifetime.

Persistence to find and bring home your loving, missing family member

First published in 2024 by Storylines Entertainment Ltd

Beara, Bantry, County Cork, Ireland P75A342
© Copyright Storylines Entertainment Ltd
and Tom Richards, 2024. All Rights Reserved

The moral right of Tom Richards to be identified as the author of this work has been asserted.

This novel is a work of fiction. The names, characters and incidents portrayed in it are the works of the author's imagination. Any resemblance to actual persons, living or dead, is entirely coincidental.

Cover by Touqeer Shahid.

Find him on fiverr.com at Touqeershahid95

Set in Times New Roman

Images courtesy of Wikipedia and other Public Sources.

Cover by *Touqeer Shahid.*

Find him on fiverr.com at Touqeershahid95

Edited by Frank McQuaid. Find him at

http://httpfrankmcquaidliteraryagency.org/

This book is sold subject to payment of the required fees. You have been granted the nonexclusive, non-transferable right to access and read the text of this book. No part of this text may be reproduced, transmitted, downloaded, decompiled, reverse engineered, stored in, or introduced into any information storage retrieval system in any form or by any means, whether electronic or mechanical, now known or hereinafter invented, without the expressed written permission of Storyline Entertainment Ltd or the author.

ISBN: 978-1-915959-42-3

Rights Acquisition: for information on rights acquisition contact

Storylines Entertainment Ltd.:

tomrichards141@gmail.com

Go to www.storylinesent.com for more information and to

purchase other books written by Tom Richards and other authors.

About This Practical Guide on Alzheimer's, Dementia and the UNFAIR Laws Across the World

This Guide is based on the TRUTH and REALITY. It is NOT a novel. The Characters in it are REAL people, though most names have been changed for obvious reasons. I have no intention of harming or insulting anyone. Carm's name and my name are, of course, real. Occasionally I use other Real names because they have either agreed to it or because they have passed away and either don't care or won't know about it. An explanation: in the title of this Guide Book, I call Carm 'my wife'. While we have not yet married due to horrible circumstances (which I will go into in many of the chapters below), calling Carm 'wife' is much less confusing than calling her 'Partner'. Some who read the title may think that 'partner' means 'Business Partner' which she is but she's much more than that. Carmel Murray is my missing, loving Legal Partner. I hope that provides an explanation.

Some will ask: " Tom, why have you written this? Won't you find it embarrassing to tell a story that is so horrible it almost made you lose your mind and you almost took your life?"

The answer, of course, is that I'm writing this Guide to prevent this from happening to anyone who reads this. That includes all those who are married, or have a partner, or a friend, or a loving colleague and are denied access to see them, usually by a relative of that loved one who is suffering from Dementia, Alzheimer's or any other grave Mental Illness (or any illness at all that requires hospitalisation or a long-term stay in a nursing home.

It is also somewhat relevant to those of you who are denied access to your children, grandchildren or great-grandchildren. That happens all the time too particularly when a son or daughter is divorced and, for reasons beyond your control, they deny you access to what could be a long list of relatives.

This Guide is based on FACTS as I know them. The medications that I describe are the results of Extensive Research on my part, and consultations with any number of doctors, psychiatrists, psychiatric nurses, legal minds and those who have been through Alzheimer's, Dementia, related illnesses or personal tragedies. Occasionally, I condense what these people have said to me during our long interviews. I do this to shorten the narrative. If I don't, this Guide could be over 1,000 pages long.

I'm going to start this way: Carm and I had a GREAT life together for, when this is published, more than 16 years. We were Happy - very much so. We were soulmates. We loved each other so much that we didn't bother to get married. We were Legal Partners and happy to stay that way - at least until I got my divorce from my Ex. I have NEVER been happier or more content in my life since the day I met Carmel Murray.

Even now, as I start this on the 7th of August, 2024, I'm surrounded by framed pictures of my 'Wife' which is what the Irish Alzheimer's Society states, categorically, that I should now call my partner - who is now in a Nursing Home (CareChoice in Trim, County Meath, Ireland). For any number of reasons that I'll go into - very stressful reasons and events - I had a heart attack because I haven't been able to see her for over two and a half years! 30 MONTHS! What would you do if you were denied access to your wife and partner for that long? I'll tell you what I did:

1. I strongly considered committing suicide. That was when Carm was first STOLEN from me without my knowledge by one of her relatives.

2. Following that, and for many, many reason, I had a near-fatal Heart Attack. I'm very lucky to be alive to write this. It's as if God has given me another chance. So now I find that I must write this Guide.

In the following Chapters, I will tell you the story, at least in part, of what happened to Carm; of what I THOUGHT was wrong with her; of the actions I took to protect her; of the actions I failed to take; of what happened to us when I first met her and how happy we both were to have found each other; of the LEGAL actions I took that were IGNORED by all the politicians and lawyers I contacted to get help for Carm; and of the fatal consequences.

I very much hope that this Guide helps. As the Title of this book states: DO NOT LET THIS HAPPEN TO YOU OR YOUR FAMILY!

In that this is a Practical Guide, I'll do my best to give readers advice on what to do, where to go, what questions to ask and how to ensure that you will always have access to your loving 'Spouse' no matter if you're partners or legally married. Finally, I'll speak my mind on what we MUST do to change laws around the world to ensure access by us, their legal partners, do those who are suffering from Alzheimer's, Dementia and similar Illnesses.

NOTE: This Writer is not a professional psychiatrist, doctor or lawyer. If you or someone you know is going through what Carm and I have over the past three years (and more), and if you fear for their lives, contact a professional Psychiatrist or a local police station. You could save someone's life - maybe your own.

"God never closes a door without opening a window."

– Anonymous (Note from Tom: This old line of Wisdom is true, isn't it? So often, as I tried to get Access to my Beloved Carmel Murray, I lost all hope. But I learned: Doors may slam in your face as you seek to answer all the questions you will have about your missing spouse or partner. But God really does push open a Window with Unseen Hands. When that happens, you'll have hope again.)

"...never was so much owned by so many to so few."

–Winston Churchill, Prime Minister of the United Kingdom, 20 August 1940.

(Note from Tom: Churchill's speech was made during the Battle of Britain. Nazi Germany was determined to invade the Southwest and West Coasts of England and turn that Royal Country into a German dominion. Here, this determined Prime Minister is talking about COURAGE. The Courage to keep going no matter what happens to you and Courage and

Chapter One

Carmel Murray's Boston Life

Carmel Dolores Murray was born on May 20, 1963 in a Trim Hospital, Trim County Meath. Her parents, Josephine Murray nee Greville and husband Tommy Murray, had four other children: in this case we'll call them boys. Their names, from the oldest to youngest child, were: Alpha, Bravo, Juliet, Golf and Carm. The family had many relatives in Trim and County Meath. One niece that I got to know well is Rose.

That's Carm's background. Two very, very loving parents and a large close-knit family. They loved and supported each other through thick and thin. For that reason, even from an early age, Carm knew she was loved. Carmel Murray went to local primary and secondary school in Trim. She stopped secondary school (High School as it's also known) at 15 years old. As she told me when we first met, "Tom, I wanted to earn my own keep. So I stopped going to school, wanting to get a well-paid job in my local town." And she did. In Trim's local drycleaners. She worked there for years until she finally went to the United States.

That was Carm, all right. Very, very independent. Also very, very intelligent despite the lack of a long formal education. So let's speed things up and it's off to Boston, MA, USA where Carm started working as a real professional, and made at least as much as I was earning at the time.

Today is 8 August 2024. Today, Carm literally disappeared from our small Village of Eyeries. Except for 20 minutes and a few seconds, I haven't really seen Carm in 2 years and 10 months. But I'll write more about this dark period of my life in another chapter.

Like any spouse or partner, I don't know every detail of Carm's life before we met. What I'm doing now is giving readers a sketch of her life - of what she told me in the many years we lived happily together.

As I understand it, Carm dated a few men in her town but couldn't find anyone she was truly attracted to. She finally started dating a farmer who lived close to her - a tall, skinny fellow who was very strong because he'd farmed most of his life. Carm dated this man (I'll call him George McGreggor after a famous Irish sports star) for a number of months. George finally proposed to Carmel Murray. In that she had no real future in Ireland at that point (there was a recession in this country then), and George lived and worked in Boston, Carm accepted only when he promised her this:

George told her that he'd help get her a job and also her Green Card. This meant that Carmel would be able to work in the United States legally. Carm told me after she divorced this absolute creep that he lied to her. So, when they both arrived in Logan Airport, Boston, and found a place to live, Carm got her own job and Green Card, without any help from her husband-to-be.

I have Carm's divorce papers in a box that I keep safe from preying eyes. I'm not going to write the date of their marriage or divorce because readers might be able to identify this male culprit and thief. What I will write is this:

Carm and George were married in a civil ceremony (not a Catholic wedding ceremony and I'm not sure why). They lived in a two-bedroom apartment in Quincy, not far from Boston City. There, Carm got herself a great paying job in a local Delicatessen that was owned by a Member of the local Mafia. To hear Carm tell this story always made me laugh. Her boss and owner of this Italian-style Restaurant, was married with a child. He and his wife loved his new employee to bits. Carmel worked as a waitress and was absolutely great at playing the 'Irish card'. The 'Joint', as her boss called it, was constantly filled with other members of the local Mafia as well as Boston cops. As they had breakfast together, Carm would fill up their coffee cups, and listen to the Police Officers discuss the possibility of arresting those Gang Members that morning in the Restaurant.

One morning, a Lieutenant with the Boston Police Force cornered Carm's Boss and told him there would be a major arrest that afternoon. Concerned for Carmel's safety, he gave her the day off. When she came home, George was under a table as they both heard sirens and gunshots outside their front window. George was shaking with fear and Carmel had to drag her then-husband out from under the table then through the front door. They sat on a small porch and watched the Police Cars, with red lights flashing, drive past their house. They were filled with arrested Gang Members. Looking at her husband who was sitting next to her, she noticed that George was as white as a sheet. Carm could only laugh. George told Carm that he knew a Member of the local Mafia who had borrowed some money from George. When that hit man didn't pay him back, George had called the cops and ratted on the entire Gang.

Carm told me many years later that in hindsight, she had married the wrong man. "Tom, he was a chicken, a thief, a liar, a gambler and he stole from me many times throughout the years. It was George who should have been arrested. That hit man was his friend and they borrowed money from each other to feed their gambling addictions."

That's Carm, too. As honest a woman as I've ever met. She did make good money at the Deli. Her boss paid her over minimum wage and the Cops gave her any change they had in their pockets as tips, and the occasional $5.00 bill. She kept all those coins and notes in a large glass jar that she hid from George. Even in the early days of their marriage, she knew that he was never to be trusted.

Now, I'm going to speed things up again and also fast-forward.

Carm started applying for much better jobs all over Boston. It took a few months but she finally landed a job in the centre of Boston. She became a Receptionist at Equity Office, then owned by Blackstone. That company was one of the largest Office Leasing companies in North America at that point. I'm so proud of my woman. After a year or so, she was not only the Receptionist. She was also the company's full-time Client Relationship Manager. She would meet the 'Big Wigs' (as she called them) at the front door and escort them in. Companies such as IBM, Microsoft and many other Blue-Chip operations rented space from Equity Office, in buildings all over the States. Often, they were seeing the Vice President of Operations for a rent review. Carm would butter them up and again played the Irish Card. She's smile, get them a Coke, tea or coffee and then escort them in to her Boss's office. Needless to say, Equity Office often increased their Client's rent. For that reason, they started giving Carm a large annual Bonus in addition to a very good monthly salary.

When I'm talking to my friends about Carmel and her time in Boston, I'll always finish by saying, "Not bad from a woman from Trim, with no real formal education, huh?" I'll smile and think about my Carm and how happy she was during those few years in the United States.

Carmel Murray became friends with most of the Staff at Equity Office. She was best friends with the President of the company, a wonderful woman I'll call Margie M. A year or so after starting work, Carm discovered that her joint bank accounts - savings and checking accounts - were often empty at the end of any month. She finally realized that George was stealing from her and, though he'd promised he would stop, was till gambling on horses.

On these many occasions, the Margie M and a few friends would give, not lend, Carm enough cash (which she took home and hid in her bedroom) to pay the rent on their new apartment (that George and Carm had both purchased) in Southie (just south of Boston City), food, utilities, and any other expenses that Carm had. George, though working at the same company (he worked in the company's underground garage), refused to contribute to the couple's monthly expenses.

When Carm moved in with me many years later, she told me that, "That George scumbag really was a thief and a liar. And you know what Tom? The day that I was diagnosed with cancer - an illness that could have taken my life - that George bum left me!" She'd always laugh at that point. "I'm so glad he did, too!"

Yep, the bum left her. But not before he took revenge on what Carm had found out about him and how much cash he'd stolen from her. George would lock her in the bathroom or their bedroom. He'd wait until she was sleeping then, opening the door, creep in and beat the living tar out of her. Carm told me that he'd make sure to hit her only in the belly, legs and arms but never in the face. That way, she could never report him to the Authorities or get him fired from his job. "George was always jealous of me because I had a much better paying job than he did," Carm told me on many occasions. "That bastard almost killed me a couple of times! But I survived despite that scum's best efforts."

(I'm 'reporting' these facts because they become VERY relevant in chapters below.)

Yes, Carm really did have cancer. She was diagnosed with a Melanoma. Her company sent her to one of the best hospitals in Boston where she "went under the knife" as Carm told me. A great surgeon operated on her. He took out all the cancer near her right knee then traced it and began to cut more out.

When he was almost finished, he cut out the lymph nodes near her crotch. Carm subsequently developed Lymphodemia which is why she limped all the time. It's also why she wore a thick, black compression stocking on her right leg. I know too well how she felt about it. That stocking was so difficult to put on each morning that I started helping her do that horrible daily task when she moved in with me.

And finally, a few other points: first, Carm eventually received her United States Citizenship and passport. She was so proud of that! She told me all about the day she took her Oath of Allegiance to the United States (she did not have to give up her Irish citizenship). Carm also divorced George the scum. She also found out that George had been "messing around", as Carm called it. George had a number of girlfriends which is one of the reasons why he kept stealing money from his legal wife. Eventually he married one who he got pregnant. Carm found out about his small secret family which is why, of course, she filed for divorce. Then, after the divorce and after Carm and I started living together, she discovered through a close friend of hers that George had divorced this second wife and married another woman! He now has two or three children with that third wife.

"What a meathead!" Carm kept telling me.

And do you know what? For years after Carm came to Eyeries and we started living together (George knew all about that, the jealous fool) he'd phone Carm on her mobile phoned and demand that she transfer cash to him to help him pay his bills.

"Are you crazy?" I can hear her saying. "You never paid me any monthly alimony ('Maintenance' in Europe) and I was the one who had to pay-off the Southie apartment mortgage. You were supposed to pay half of that, weren't you Mister George? That's what the judge ruled and I have it in writing! But you, you scumbag, now you can't even hold down a full-time job!" Then she'd hang up on him and both laugh like hell. "Tom, it's great to finally get even," she'd tell me after those brief conversations. "Yep," I'd reply. "Remember, as they say in many films, 'Revenge is best served very, very cold!'"

And so it is! And one day, if Carm and I are very, very fortunate, we'll get our revenge on those who have tried their very best to kill both of us.

Chapter Two:

A Meeting We Weren't Expecting

Every now and then, the male of this human species gets very, very lucky. In May, 2009, I had one of the luckiest chance meetings I've ever experienced.

I write this to show you how grateful to God I am to have met the most important woman in my life: Carmel Dolores Murray. And when I write 'chance', I mean it!

I had decided to visit my father. At that point, and a year after my mother had passed away in a Florida Hospice, Dad bought a really wonderful two-bedroom apartment to the South of Tampa. He was very, very happy there. I had been travelling back and forth to visit my parents since 1982 when I moved permanently to Ireland. This time, in May 2009, I boarded a United Airlines flight in Dublin and flew non-stop to Tampa International Airport. Dad and I visited for ten days and on May 24 (four days after Carm's birthday) I flew from Tampa to Boston's Logan International Airport where I would take a United flight back to Dublin, via Shannon airport.

Now here's the thing and the truth: I could have chosen many airports to fly from Tampa and onward to Dublin. That first flight could have been through ORD in Chicago, Newark Airport, JFK, Atlanta or a few others. But the flights to all of these other airports were full so I had to choose Boston.

I well remember that when I landed in Boston I had a four-hour layover. I decided to go to the gate and there started a new John Grisham novel. After an hour sitting on my bum, I looked around and saw a really nice bar: Boston Bruins Bar. I bought a bottle of Sam Adams and, sitting down at the table, started to read again. Now get this: years later, Carm told me that she'd been sitting at a table quite close to where I was sitting. She noticed this "American Yank" as she called me, sipping his beer directly from the bottle and reading. I guess I was dressed rather well. She told me that I looked very attractive to her.

Carm had come to the terminal early. She'd woken up late because the office staff had given her a going away party (Carm was flying back to Ireland to visit her parents). She had a beer and then the boarding announcement was made for our flight. She followed me to the gate and stood in line right behind me. When we finally boarded the flight, we were both sitting in economy. I had seat 36A. Carm had seat 37C. I sat down and again started reading my novel. As I read, sipping a glass of water, this absolutely gorgeous woman sat right beside me. She smiled at me and, closing her eyes, pretended that she was asleep. A woman came up and tapped Carm on the shoulder. "Sorry," the woman said showing Carm her boarding pass. "But that's my seat."

Carm shook her head. "No it's not. It's mine. See?" She showed the woman part of her boarding pass. The woman frowned.

"Young woman, that is MY seat! Your seat is probably right behind this one."

The flight attendant came up to the woman to see what was wrong. As the woman explained, Carm looked over at me and winked. At that point I was absolutely hooked! I could tell she was Irish immediately, but not where from of course. She had the best-looking eyes I'd ever seen: hazel. Her hair was auburn. She had a little elfin face. As the flight attendant and the woman, both standing in the aisle quite near us, kept talking, Carm stuck her hand out. "I'm Carm Murray but you can call me Pookey. Everyone I know does."

"Pookey Murray?" I asked as I shook her warm hand. "My name is Tom Richards."

We kept shaking hands for some time. I knew in my heart that I'd found the woman of my dreams. Then we both noticed that the woman had sat down in Carm's seat right behind us and we were delighted.

"It's going to be a very short flight," I said to her. "So, we have hours together. Tell me about yourself, Pookey?"

And she did. Not much, of course, but enough. I won't go into the details of that first flight together, but as I always told Carm for years and years, "Pook, that was the best flight I've ever had! What a miracle."

Sitting beside each other on our living room couch and sipping a glass of wine, she'd wink at me. "Yes it was. The best miracle flight of our lives."

We knew that should we be lucky enough to have children and grandchildren, it would be a story that was told for many years: of how a lonely man from Ireland (originally from the United States) and a lonely woman from the States (originally from Ireland) were fortuitous enough to meet each other.

Carm, of course, had to go back to Boston after two weeks in County Meath. At that point, I had left my wife, the former Mrs Richards. Pookey and I kept in touch by email and with an occasional phone call. A year later, and because her parents were getting older, Carmel Dolores Pookey Murray made the huge decision to come home to Ireland.

And that was the luckiest phone call and email I've ever received from anyone in my entire life. I remember thinking: "That's it! We'll be married soon!"

That didn't happen. Not right then. And now, due to Pook's Dementia, perhaps not forever. But maybe. Just maybe. After all, a huge amazing miracle happened when I met Carm. Maybe, just maybe, Carm and I will both be given another one.

Chapter Three

The Loving Partnership Unfolds

Condensing almost fifteen years together is very difficult. If you've been married (or have been with a partner) for as long as Carm and I have been together, we could all write any number of books and Guides to tell people about our loving relationships. Like any couple, Carm and I would disagree at times. Or we could have arguments about certain things. But we always, always made up before we went to sleep together.

What I'm doing here is explaining how much Carm and I love each other. How we supported and took care of each other when we went through difficulties in life together. Of how close we were. Carm and I were best friends. We were more than soulmates. Looking back on our relationship I finally realize: Carm and I could have been twins, we were that close. We thought alike. We'd finish each other's sentences when we were discussing things. We dressed somewhat alike. We liked similar foods, drinks, dancing together, the sea, our Village home, each other's relatives, the weather. One thing's for sure, Carm and I never ran out of things to talk about. We were that close.

Now that she's gone from my life, at least for right now, I look around and could swear I hear her constantly whispering to me. It's as if she's talking to me inside my head. Every night she touches my heart with her prayers. She kisses my cheek at night and in the morning. I dream about her constantly. At first, when they first stole her from me, I had nightmares about my best girl. She was either dead, couldn't remember me or was over ninety years old and in a wheelchair. But now, and because I've hired a lawyer to fight for both Carm and me and our mutual rights to be with each other, I have only good dreams.

When I left my Ex-wife (we were finally divorced only a few months ago – that's another story. It has to do with the Catholic Church in Ireland, the closing of the courts in this country due to Covid, the fact that Carm and I didn't have to be legally married to consider ourselves husband and wife and due to the simple fact that my Ex and I kept arguing about money – which Carm knew was hurtful to me – for all of those reasons Carm and I never married which is a true sin) I first moved to an apartment in Trim which is yet another miracle.

Carm and I exchanged telephone numbers and email addresses but we never bothered to share addresses. I had no idea at all where lived – it could have been anywhere near Dublin Ireland. But when I signed the rental agreement for that really nice 2-bed apartment, I emailed Carm the address. She phoned me instantly.

"In Trim, Tom? You're kidding! I was born in Trim. My parents live in Trim only a half-mile from your apartment building."

When I put down the phone I couldn't believe what she'd told me. I mean, I could have rented anywhere close to Dublin and my children. If you look at a good map of Dublin and Meath Counties on the

East Coast of Ireland, you'll see how fortunate I am. I was considering at least six to eight different small towns just northwest of Dublin City to call my new home. But Trim? It's as if I'd shot an arrow into the sky and, pushed by an unseen hand, it landed in the hometown of my future partner. It was that fortuitous for both Carm and me.

Before Carm came back to Ireland permanently, she invited me to visit her in Boston. Which is exactly what I did. The first time I visited, I landed in Logan, picked up a rental car, and followed Carm's written instructions to the apartment (that she now stayed in on her own with her great little white dog, Jack) in Braintree, MA (in the Southie area). This is the one that Carm and her Ex had bought together. And what a great time we had during my ten-day stay with her! I got to know Jack the Dog very well. I helped Carm to feed him. We took the car into Boston City (that was the first time I'd been there in well over thirty years - I have relatives living in Lowell, not far from the City, and some of my ancestry is from Plymouth Rock) and I took Carm out to dinner not once but many times. She'd always take me out for lunch. We walked through Boston, hand in hand, in the good summer weather. We wandered through Boston Common and then took the Tram as far as it travelled in both directions. She took me to Little Italy and bought me my first real Cannoli. She took my picture in front of Paul Revere sitting on his horse and I took one of Carm standing in front of that mighty revolutionary statue. We went to the bar made famous by the hit television series, 'Cheers' and had lunch inside, then a drink outside at a table where we both had a cigarette. She took me to Fenway Park but it was off-season so we couldn't enjoy a baseball game.

Carm took me to lunch at a huge Boston hotel and then her phone rang. It was the President of her company saying that she had reserved a large room on the 7th floor for us. That night, dinner and a bottle of champagne were 'on the house'.

Man, did Carm and I enjoy that night. It was as if we were on our Honeymoon. We had a great room with a balcony overlooking Boston Harbour. We were so close to Logan that, at night, we had to close the balcony doors due to the noise of the landing aircraft.

The next morning, after breakfast, she again took my hand and we took a walk right past Equity Office's Headquarters Building. She took me into her favourite large Catholic Church, two blocks from where she worked, and she explained all of the stained-glass windows to me. We both prayed at the Statue of Saint Anthony, the Saint of lost souls which, even now, is her favourite Saint. We both lit candles for our families and those who had died, and gave a dollar each to a poor homeless man who was sitting just outside the Church.

My memory of that trip is so vivid it's as if I'm reliving it as I type this. The second trip, only a few months later, was just as exciting and as wonderful. I again stayed with Carm in her Boston apartment. Jack and I became even closer. We took a walk to a nearby Shopping Centre and there I took Carm into the Sayers Jewelry Store. The memory of those few minutes is burned into this man's head. I talked to the sales assistant as Carm stood just behind me. She couldn't hear me but I'd asked him for a selection of Emerald Rings. When he came out with the tray, Carm asked me, "Tom, what on earth are you doing?"

"Nothing, sweetie. You'll see. Now, why don't you try a few on?"

You should have seen Carm blush. These weren't engagement rings. I couldn't afford a large diamond ring back then. But the rings were all perfect. The blue of the stone matched the glint in Carm's hazel eyes. She picked one that had a large blue stone and diamond chips. It has a gold setting. When she tried it on it fit perfectly. Holding it up so both of us could see it, she started to cry.

"Tom, are you asking me to marry you?"

"Damned right I am," I said as I got on my knees. "Will you Carm Murray take me..."

As the sales assistant began to applaud, Carm started to laugh. "Of course I do! But you need to get legally divorced first, you know."

"Which I will as soon as possible," I promised. "But for now..."

"We'll have to be legal partners which means that we're married in the eyes of God."

Which is exactly what happened, as far as Carm, God and Tom are concerned. But many, many people don't believe it and never will.

After that first proposal, Carm and I drove down to New York City. She'd never been there and had always wanted to go but never had the cash. So I took her. "My treat!" I insisted as we planned that amazing trip of a lifetime.

We drove all the way down to New York City, stopping at every Rest Stop that we saw. There, we'd both go to the toilet and get something out of a vending machine. We might buy some little thing at one of the small tourist shops. Stopping at Rest Stops became a tradition with Carm and me. Anytime we went to the States together and drove down a Freeway, we'd make a 'Pit Stop'. We had such a great time travelling together.

New York City was a BLAST! The best damned two-night holiday of my life, Carm would later say. We stayed in the Fitzgerald Hotel just off Times Square and had dinner or a drink in what seemed to be every Irish Bar we saw. Both nights, we'd walk arm-in-arm into Times Square and Carm would marvel at all the lights. During the mornings, we'd hang out our bedroom window (we couldn't get a room with a Balcony) and Carm would pretend it was Thanksgiving. "Someday, Tom, I want to come back here to see the Macy's Thanksgiving Parade."

We never made it. And maybe someday? Who knows. Carm, in her state of dementia, might well know. But she's keeping that a secret! Hah! And don't I wish it would all come true.

After she moved back to Ireland in early 2010, she and I lived together in that 2-bed apartment. Oh, what a wonderful time! Three days a week she would stay with her parents. The rest of those precious days were for Carm and me. It was as if we were dating. We'd walk into Trim and have a drink and split some appetisers at the Trim Castle Hotel. We'd sit at the window and, because it was summer, watch the Hot Air Balloons float over the hotel from a field just beyond

Trim Castle, which was just across the street. We might drive up to see her best friend (I'll call her X Ray here, and what a brilliant friend she still is to Carm) and after a great visit, go back to our apartment together.

Those months flash before my eyes like a dream. We had a great time in that apartment and really got to know each other. Then, a few months after first moving in, I made the decision to move down to Eyeries, County Cork.

Carm at first couldn't believe it. "Where? How far south?"

"Seven hours, Pook," I replied. "Come on, you'll love it."

I'd made the decision to buy where we both now live well before Carm came home permanently. I hadn't told her about it because I was still negotiating with the owner and so hadn't closed the deal. But when I told her, the owner and I had come to a deal and I'd have the keys to the house in only a few weeks.

The drive down was great fun. Carm had never been to County Cork. Because Carm never had a driving license in Ireland (she drove in the U.S. and I eventually gave her a gift of driving lessons when she moved permanently to Eyeries) she'd sit back and watch all the cows in the fields. When we came finally to Cashel, County Limerick, we stopped for a late lunch in the local McDonalds. This became another tradition of ours. Every time we drove up to see her family, we'd stop at McD's and have a Big Mac, fries and a coffee or a Coke.

When we arrived in Eyeries, she couldn't take her eyes off the homes in the beautiful Village. I had stopped to get the key from the local Auctioneer who had negotiated the deal for me, and opening the front door, let Carm go in first. She looked around the small furnished cottage and I could tell she was falling in love with it.

"In many ways, it's like the home I grew up in, Tom," she said as I took her upstairs to what would become our bedroom. "It's just as warm and cozy and not too big. What's it like out in the garden?"

I took her downstairs again and opened the back door. "What an amazing view!" she said smiling up at me. "I love this view! But Tom, this village is so remote I don't think I could ever live here with you."

"You're the most honest woman I've ever met," I replied, kissing her gently on the cheek. "Carm, I have to live here. I've always wanted to live on the coast and near the water and this place is the only home I can afford. Please consider it. Live here with me."

She nodded her head and, after locking up the house, walked back up the narrow main street to Causkey's Bar for a drink. As we sat at the table, she smiled again. "Tom, I've considered it," she said as she looked around the room. "I love all the local people I've talked to in here. They're all wonderful!" She took my hand. "As you know, I came home to Ireland to take care of Mam and Dad. How about if we arrange it so that I come down for a visit every few weeks to be with you and you come up to me in the same way?"

Which is exactly what we both did. Eventually, two years after that first visit to Eyeries, Carm's parents passed away. I went up in my pickup and we loaded many of her clothes as well as Jack into the big blue car. When we got back to Eyeries, and when she got out of the car, I handed her a set of keys to the house. She looked at the keys sitting in her little hand.

"Home?" she asked, looking up at me. "Really? It's my home, too?"

I closed her fingers around the keys. "Home. As long as you're here, this will no longer be a house. It will be our home."

Now Pook is gone to a nursing home with Dementia. I look around and see, many hours each day, only a house. Sometimes, though, mostly at night, when she's whispering to me, I swear I can see her and little Jack in bed next to me.

Maybe it's the delusion of a tired, grieving mind. I'm not sure. What I do know is that occasionally, I feel the warmth of Jack as he curls up at my feet like he always did and Carm as she hugs me first then kisses me before I reach over and turn the lights out. We'd say some prayers together and soon, all three of us had gone fast asleep.

"Goodnight Carm," I whisper to her pillow every night. "Sweet dreams," I say to the picture that rests on the locker next to her head.

"Goodnight, Tom," she'd reply. "Sleep well and God Bless."

But now I've been denied access to my legal partner. Which is a Nightmare beyond belief. I have trouble saying prayers for her relatives or friends anymore. Why should I when they've damned Carm to a prison called a nursing home and damned me to a hell not of my making but of theirs?

And that is the subject of the rest of this Guide. Why?? Why did they do what they did and what can I do to counter their actions and see my legal partner and wife?

"Why?" you may ask at this point. "Why would they do that to you and Carm when they all knew how much you both loved each other.

"Why?" I answer. "I have no idea. To be frank, I don't care anymore. Answering that single word question is no longer a problem. Besides, I know the answer to that. And it isn't very pleasant.

Which is another part of this Guide. The answer: "Why" isn't a question. It means nothing at all to me anymore. You'll find out 'why' very, very soon.

Chapter Four

Where is my (Insert Relationship and Name)????

Answer: Often, no one will tell you.

> Guideline Number 1
> <u>Keep asking important questions.</u> The Answer are often Confusing and Stupid Beyond Belief. And usually, those answering your questions are lying to you. Or, all you'll hear from them is SILENCE.

Guideline Number 1 is based on personal experience. Since Carm was stolen from our home in Eyeries (and from my life) I've asked many people critical and urgent questions concerning her locations and health. Some of these vital questions include but are not limited to (and I still ask people these questions and press them for answers which I've occasionally received):

- Where is Carmel? I haven't seen her in (put in the number of months or years). Do you know if she's alive or dead? Please! Answer me (the usual answer is overwhelming silence).

- What's wrong with Carmel? Does she have a brain tumour? Does she have PTSD? Has she been run over by a truck? WHAT THE HELL IS WRONG WITH HER? Why doesn't she answer her mobile phone or email me. She always, always did (when I ask this to a relative or professional on my mobile phone, I'll get through to them. They'll ask, "Hello, who is this?" When I reply, "It's Tom. You know, Tom Richards. We've known each other for well over fifteen years!" Then, all I hear is a 'click' as the other party hangs up.

- What is her diagnosis? Okay, let's assume that you finally find your loved one. They're in a nursing home or a hospital far away from you. You ask if you can come up to see them, but you discover that you don't have access at all. You are certain they'll answer this simple question. And they do! But they'll often lie to you.

- In my case, this one question resulted in a number of answers from the Receptionist (or a Nurse) in Carm's Nursing Home. The answers were:

- "She has Covid so you can't see her we're afraid." Or,

- "I'm sorry but everyone upstairs is working or off-duty. They'll phone you back soon to answer that question." Do they ever? No.

- "Mister Richards, you're only Carmel Murray's Partner so you have NO RIGHT AT ALL to know what's troubling our patient. You'd best ask either a relative or the Alzheimer's Society of Ireland." (CLICK. They hang up)

- "Hi Mister Richards. This is Carm's Nurse. I take care of her during the day." (Me thinking, "Finally!") "Carm is doing very well. She's eating well and talking to our other residents. She can't come to the phone right now but I'll tell her you called. She probably won't phone you back. She doesn't really phone anyone anymore or take phone calls for that matter." Me: "Thanks so much, Nurse, for taking my call. You're the first one in the Nursing home to talk to me in, what? Well over a year?"

- "Mister Richards, I mean Tom, Carm really does remember you."

- "Honest?

- "Honest. I'm not lying. She asks about you all the time. I'd better get back to work now. Bye!" (Me thinking to myself and punching the air with joy: "Finally, someone will actually talk to me?

But what about her diagnosis? Here we go again folks. The answers from various professionals that I've talked to about Carm.

"We're not certain. It could be absolutely anything." "We THINK it's Alzheimer's but it could be a brain tumour." "We're certain it has to do with the medication Carm's on for Rheumatism."
"Look, Mister Richards, Carm is here only for a month or so. She needed some time to think about you and what she wants to do with the rest of her life." (Me, to this stupid man: "She told me what she wants to do. We're going to get married!") Him: "That's not what she told us! She told us to... (CLICK, he hangs up)."
"Tom, I'm Jane Doe. I'm Carmel Murray's Alzheimer's Advocate. I know you've been trying to find out what Carm's diagnosis is. So hear this when I tell you: YOU ARE NOT ALLOWED TO GO NEAR HER. YOU CAN'T TALK TO HER. YOU'LL NEVER LEARN ANYTHING ABOUT HER. YOU'LL NEVER SEE HER AGAIN. PERIOD!!! (CLICK)"

Finally, about four months ago (more when this is finally published) I received a letter from my Solicitor who is trying to get me access to Carm at her Nursing home. The letter, which had been dictated to another Solicitor by Carmel's sister who is her Next of Kin was a number of pages long. But one paragraph had Carm's diagnosis. As I read it for the first time, I punched the air and shouted (though no one was around to hear me). "HALLELUIA! Finally! A real diagnosis.

Carm has, I'm fairly sure, *frontotemporal dementia*- FTD - the same disease that American Actor Bruce Willis has. When this sister wrote that to me, all of the pieces of the jigsaw came together. I'll run through that in the next chapter of how I started to realise that something was wrong with Carm, of the few actions I took and of what I <u>*did not do*</u> (and I have berated myself over and over again for what I did not do. Man, was I a foolish, foolish Legal Partner).

Other Questions I've asked repeatedly

- Can I visit Carm at the Nursing home? Answer: No (except for 1 time a few years ago)

- Will Carm be able to come home to Eyeries at some point? Answer: Silence

- What's her treatment? What are her medications? Answer: Silence

- Is she eating and sleeping? Answer: Silence

- WHEN CAN I SEE HER!?! Answer: NEVER! GO AWAY OR WE'LL ARREST YOU!

- Has another Psychiatrist visited Carm to give a second opinion regarding her diagnosis? Answer: Silence

- (When I started to feel VERY, VERY unwell due to the stress of NOT knowing the answers to any of the above questions, an Important

Question to my Own Doctor): Doctor, I need an appointment right now! I'm having pains in my chest and I can't breath for some reason. Answer: "Sorry, I'm too busy right now. I'll call back later today or a nurse will." Me: "But my chest really Hurts!" Doctor: Sorry. We'll call you back. (Did they ever phone back? Answer: no. Subsequent Problem: Tom Richards had an almost fatal heart attack in April, 2022. Yes, all of you who read this. I almost DIED! But did I? Of course not. And someday, I'll get even for the problems that all of these Lunatic so-called Doctors did to me. All they did was denied the Oath that they Swore: The Hippocratic Oath! That's all they did. (NOTE: health problems happen to many, many people who are denied access to their partners, spouse, friends or relatives. Some as you well know commit suicide because they see no light at the end of any tunnel. Not a glimmer of hope that they'll ever again see the person(s) they love with all their heart.

- (From two close friends: one is a retired Psychiatric Nurse. The other is a Director of Nursing at a Memory Care Centre somewhere in Florida) If I can get access to Carm, if that ever happens, is there anything I can do to reverse her memory loss? Or at least to halt that memory loss? Answers: Yes, of course there is. In the United States, there are a number of medications and Therapies that have been approved recently by the FDA (U.S. Food and Drug Administration) which may never be available in Ireland or Europe. Get her over here, Tom, ASAP. This will not only help Carm to reverse her decline in memory loss; she will be able to talk to you, love you again, and extend her life by a countless number of years. (NOTE: the two people above, who shall stay nameless to protect their identities, have met Carm a number of times. They are certain of my love for her and are the only two psychiatric professionals that I know who are willing to give me and my lawyer a signed and sworn Affidavit. NONE of the psychiatrists that I know in Ireland have met Carmel Murray. Which means that an Affidavit from these people – though they would be willing if I asked them – would be useless in a Court of Law.

The above Questions are not, of course, the only questions I've asked. The Big one, the most relevant one, that I've asked is this: If I really am Carmel Murray's Legal Partner, what rights do I have?

The answers from legal professionals vary considerably. Some say that I, as a partner, have no legal rights at all (which is very, very depressing). Others say that I have some legal rights. For instance, I can change my will to include Carm so that she will be financially secure when I die (I've done that). If we, as partners that live together, separate, both of us have equal rights to our joint assets and any debt that we have. Should we have children, we also have rights to fight for visitation and / or making them legal dependents. We also have a right to fight for Alimony (Maintenance) should one of us be wealthier than the other.

The one that really made me feel hopeful (about a year to 18 months ago) was a speech that I attended given by an Alzheimer's Society of Ireland Advocate (at that point, I thought this person was my Advocate - but they weren't! As a man who has no Alzheimer's or Dementia (thank the Lord) I am not entitled to an Advocate). This person stood up and said: "As a legal partner you have many, many rights. The term, 'Next of Kin' is a convenience for the medical profession. It has no legal basis whatsoever. You, as legal partners, are their 'legal next of kin' and are their Legal Guardian."

I was so relieved when I heard that person say that. So much so that I stood up and applauded. Unfortunately, 'Legal Guardianship' at least in Ireland has no real 'legal meaning or definition'.

In Ireland as in many countries, politicians, doctors, psychiatrists, some Alzheimer's Advocates and some relatives of those with the disease have worked to change the law. In Ireland as in many countries throughout the world, the laws were ancient and worked to protect the doctors and staff, not the patients or their legal partners.

Chapter Five

Why Laws Must Change Across the World to Protect those Suffering from Mental Illnesses and Their Legal Partners

> Guideline Number 2
> Understand the Relevant Laws in Your Country regarding Legal Guardianship, Next of Kin, Legal Decision Makers, Power of Attorney, Wills, and Various Healthcare Acts.
>
> Prior to Carm's hospitalisation, we didn't and I very much regret it.

As I wrote at the very beginning of this Guide, I am not a lawyer, solicitor or barrister. I did study some law in the United States as an Undergraduate Student, and a small bit of law when I was studying for my MBA at UCLA. I do know how to write a legal brief (I worked in Washington, D.C. as a legislative analyst and also for a large county government in Central Illinois). But am I a qualified lawyer in any country? Answer: Not on your life! And the problem is: my life as well as Carm's (and possibly your own life and the life of your legal partner) could depend on finding a good lawyer to help you.

The first problem: for reasons I don't understand, in most Western countries there is a shortage of lawyers. I've tried to get professional legal help to access Carm since the month that she was stolen from me. Most of the lawyers that I talk to here are either too busy, under-staffed or are at the point of retiring. For all of those reasons, I decided to study the law – those that are relevant – to help me answer some of my own questions about my own legal rights.

This is a very brief synopsis of what I've found.

First a brief background of mental health acts, very old ones. I'll use Ireland as an example but they apply in most countries.

The Lunacy Act (1871) – see https://www.irishstatutebook.ie/eli/1871/act/22/enacted/en/print.html was an act that was designed to replace all related Mental Health Laws in this country that had been passed prior to that year. The name of the act tells it all at least to me. 'Lunacy' means that you are absolutely crackers when, according to this law, you may be absolutely mentally fit. I read the entire act a few years ago and was amazed. In this act, ordering and arresting people to go into an 'insane asylum' was fairly standard. Drunks, those who were having moments of exhaustion, those deemed 'mentally unwell' by relatives (usually because those relatives were fighting over an inheritance. The easiest way to get rid of that 'competitor' for a farm, land or house, was to phone the local police and ask them to arrest your competitor. Simple as that. No proof of lunacy required) even though there was no proof as to mental incompetence, people here who refused to go to Mass as ordered by the local priest were thrown into an Asylum; prostitutes, gay people – pick someone! If you were considered 'abnormal' by a friend or neighbour, into the local Asylum you might go! Despite your protests to the local authorities. And once in? You had little chance of getting out unless you had access to a relative or friend with a great deal of cash. Then you could bribe your way out.

'Sectioning' as it was called back then, was in common use. No 'law' was required for you to section anyone you know or might know or possibly knew. This single Act was one of the worst mental health acts passed by any legislature in the world. In this act, no one had any rights except those who pointed fingers at someone they wanted 'legally incarcerated'.

"My sister is crazy! She says that I've stolen all of her money! We are contesting our dead parents' will in court and I think she's cracked up. I'll try to work it all out with her over a cup of tea. But she is crazy! I found a stash of £500 in her mattress! I'm actually worried that she'll murder me. The woman has a shotgun concealed under the bed. The last time I went into her bedroom she pointed at me, cocked the triggers and threated to shoot me dead!"

That's not a real quote. It's based on a number of legal documents that I read and quotes from those people entering a Police Station and accusing a friend or relative (usually) of lunatic behaviour. Note how the Accusor sounds so reasonable and how he paints his sister as absolutely nuts. More research indicates that, in the above example, the Brother was the one who belonged in the Asylum. But that didn't happen, of course. The Brother was a man! The sister a woman. And men were listened to more than women ever were. (This still happens all over the world – men paint women as 'cat's' or crazy or lesbian or whatever without any proof. The accused won't go to an Asylum but those out-of-control accusations can tarnish their reputations, depending on what they do and where they live).

The above sister in that quote has no chance to defend herself. She can't afford a lawyer (£500 was never found in her mattress. That was a fabrication) and she doesn't have a trial. She's dragged from her cottage, her home, by the local Police and thrown into the Asylum. Often, back then, she has no chance of getting out. Not ever! In fact, it's a death sentence imposed on her by no legal judge at all (this still happens today around the world. Why the law MUST be changed).

This law was replaced, finally, by the Mental Health Act 2001. That act was much the same as the Lunacy Act 1871 but had some important differences. For the first time, patients had legal rights.

As an example (and most Western Countries have similar laws so read carefully) let's say that you're walking down the street. You've had a really, really stressful day. You sit down on a park bench, in good weather, and pull out a small bottle of whisky. No one is around, so you take a sip or two. You reflect on what's happened in the past few years: of how your father and mother passed away unexpectedly and how you miss them; of the divorce that you went through and the fact that the court ruled that you can't see your kids without supervision (despite the fact that you supported them for years and was always more than kind to them). You're a nice person. You feed the pigeons in this park every single day.

So, you're sitting there and along comes your General Practitioner. She sees you start to cry. She knows you've had many difficulties recently and she's convinced that not only will you commit suicide but you'll also murder your former wife. So concerned is your Doctor that she calls the local Police (Garda Siochana in Ireland) and tells them that you are a threat to yourself and others. She fills in a single form, has a Police staff member sign it and sends it to the local Psychiatric Unit.

Finished crying, you pick yourself up off the bench, brush yourself off, put the bottle back in your pocket (you only took two sips and you never ever drink alcohol) and stumble out of the park. As you cross the street without looking, your almost hit by a taxi who screeches to a stop. Your Doctor watches while the Taxi Driver screams at you to be more careful.

So what happens next to this poor man sitting on the park bench. Here's what happens, very often, in this kind of situation. Today, it's called Involuntary Admission. The poor guy wakes up at 7:30 AM as usual and is getting ready for work. He has a robe on and nothing else under it. As he starts to dress, he hears a loud bang on his front door. Opening it, three staff members from the local Psychiatric Unit as well as a member of the Police march in, grab him and whisk him to the Unit. Under lock and key, I might add! You see, that poor man is considered a threat to his own life until he can prove his innocence – which happens often today, thank God. At the Psychiatric Unit he's given a Mental Health Examination. If he doesn't pass it (which happens very often – they're rather easy to fail) – he is incarcerated without benefit of a trial or a lawyer being present. The man has lost his human rights. All of them! In an instant!

His General Practitioner and the Unit Psychiatrist deem him mentally unfit. In this case, they both state in a written legal document that, "Mister Joe Bloggs is suffering from Alcoholism, Schizophrenia, Hypertension, Grandiosity and a wide variety of other mental health issues. We recommend that he be committed to the Psychiatric Unit for a period of three (3) months."

That's exactly what happens! For three whole months that poor man will sit in a small room and slowly go crazy. Though his friends and other family members are certain that he's completely sane, he'll be surrounded by the truly mentally insane (or those who are there for observation). He'll be force to take a wide range of medication (most of which can result in a desire to commit suicide - read the small print!). He'll sit in his room and try to read a book. He won't have a belt to hang himself with so suicide isn't an option. He'll finally think of an idea that could help him! He'll phone a friend (he's allowed to bring his Mobile Phone into his room) and ask him to recommend a good lawyer. The friend gives him the number of the lawyer. A phone call later, the lawyer suddenly appears and tells the Psychiatrist that what they've done is illegal and a breach of law. Which it is! The poor man is let out the next day and subsequently sues EVERYONE involved. And usually, he'll win! Thank God.

Often, of course, men and women and occasionally someone in their late teens will be Involuntarily Committed for their own good. Take a friend of mine. We'll call him Tim. A great man, he went through hell for over a year. His small business failed. He owed many bills. Because of his apparent 'failure' as a father and husband, his wife left him. Tim didn't drink one drop of alcohol and was determined never to start, even when his life looked hopeless. One day, late at night in a rental apartment, he considered taking his life. Instead, the next morning he rang a local Psychiatric Unit who suggested that he come into the Unit for a Mental Health Exam.

Tim is a very, very intelligent man but when he arrived at the Unit, and despite his great effort to fail, he failed the exam. As in F A I L. The Psychiatrist on duty suggested to Tim that he stay for a week or so for observation. Tim objected vehemently. He tried to leave the Unit but the door was locked. Because Tim had told the Psychiatrist that he had considered taking his own life, that bright Psych guy committed Tim against his new patient's wishes. Involuntary Admission but this time for very good reason.

The difference here is that Tim already had a good lawyer. When the lawyer came to see him and interviewed the Psychiatrist, both of them realized that the Patient Tim was in the right place. The lawyer told Tim that he had rights. Great ones! In three months, and so this new law states, Tim has the right to appeal his Involuntary Admission at a Tribunal that takes place in or near the Unit. His lawyer can represent him.

When three months had passed, and at the Tribunal, Tim and his lawyer convinced the judge and the independent lawyers that were present that he was again mentally fit. Tim walked out of the Unit. No record appears on any of Tim's public files. All of that is, according to the law, marked CONFIDENTIAL.

The above example is true not only in Ireland but many countries across the world. Moreover, if Tim had been unable to convince the Tribunal of his mental wellness, he is entitled to another Tribunal. Then another and another until he's mentally fit and allowed to leave the Psychiatric Unit.

I've written about this new law in the case of ordinary people but how does it apply to those suffering from Alzheimer's, Dementia and other mental illnesses. Well, in my experience, it does and it doesn't.

I've provided some examples of this new Law for this very simple reason: YOU as a legal partner, spouse or friend might become so upset that you break this new law or the laws in your country of residence. One thing I've learned and it's this: We all have our breaking points. I'll admit it - when Carm was stolen from me and I couldn't find her I went insane with Grief. I DID consider suicide but I didn't do it. Instead, I had a heart attack! And I survived that. Then many more horrible things happened to me that also affected Carm. My stress levels once again went off the scale. I had difficulties breathing again. My balance became uncertain. Despite a great deal of exercise and a good diet (which my Heart Surgeon strongly recommended), I could feel as weak as a kitten.

What a Psychiatrist told me is this: Grief is a load that you can't share alone. Your body will feel heavy - very heavy. You'll have trouble concentrating and focusing. You'll be unsteady on your feet. Your head will be filled with Carm and her memory unless and until you share it by getting professional help.

Which is exactly what I did and continue to do. I won't go into the detail - it's too long. But I went to family therapy, Grief Therapy, Online counselling and finally Psychological Grief Therapy. I still have a long journey ahead of me. But by sharing what I feel, think and believe with someone (one of the reasons I'm writing this Guide) I can share at last! Almost everything! I can be honest again and feel like I'm sharing to my Carm. What a relief to share; to know that you're being heard and you can talk because your counsellor has not only experienced at least some of what you're going through but is highly qualified.

That's why, at the very very beginning of this Guide, I write in part: "If you or someone you know is suffering from (make your own list here) seek immediate professional help. Remember, your actions could not only save someone's life - BUT YOUR OWN.

And that is so very true.

I'll end this chapter by going back to Carm and those suffering the same illnesses.

In the case of a nursing home and most patients, and I reiterate, they have no legal rights at all. In some ways, their admission is like the old 'Sectioning'. They are brought in, interviewed, and placed in a ward. They're given medication if they need it or if it's been prescribed. But from that point on, their life is not their own to live. And maybe: NEVER AGAIN.

For all I know, because I have no access, Carmel Dolores Murray is FULLY mentally fit. She's in there Involuntarily but has no right to get out. Here, I'll give two examples. The first one is 'fiction' and based on my imaginings. The second is perfectly true.

Let's assume that Carm was living with her great Aunt. The aunt didn't like Carm at all but was forced, due to her own Dementia, to have someone live with her. She disliked Carm so much that she rang her Doctor and told that man that Carmel Murray was threatening her with a knife. Late at night, she'd run down the Main Street of the town completely naked, screaming obscenities and throwing rocks at statutes because, Carm told her, the statues moved. Therefore, the woman said, blowing hard into her handkerchief, Carm believes that statues all move! And it's true! she concludes.

The Doctor doesn't know Carm at all. But fully believing that she has Dementia, she has Carm picked up by the local Police and taken to the nearest Nursing Home. There, Carm is given a tranquilizer and falls asleep. That night, a nurse gives Carm another tranquiliser only stronger this time. When Carm wakes in the morning, the nurse give Carm an even stronger tranquilizer. When the doctor finally examines her that day, Carm is so confused and apparently drunk that the Doctor, a fully qualified psychiatrist, gently tells Carm that she's staying there for a few months. "Observation only," the doctor says as he leaves.

What Carm doesn't realize is that her wise old Aunt declared herself Carm's next of kin to her doctor. When the Police took Carm into their Police Car, the doctor told the cop that was driving that the Aunt was Carm's next of kin. Carm will not be able to get out of the nursing home until the Aunt, her legal Next of Kin, says that Carm can leave or Carm hires a good lawyer and proves that she's mentally fit enough to leave the nursing home.

That's where we come in people. We may not be legal next of kin but we are legal partners or wives, husbands and what have you. The people in nursing homes who are being held there against their will are depending on us to get them out. All we have to do is prove that they are competent enough to live at home with us.

The last example, a true story. I have a close friend who has a brother. The brother, who lives quite far from me, was his Uncles 'keeper'. The Uncle was getting older - only 67 or so - and was slowing down considerably. The Brother thought that the uncle was a pain in the Butt. Let's call the Uncle: William. William would start to scream at the Brother (Bob) for tea or coffee it the morning. "Bob, get your fat ass in here! I need my coffee right now!" Bob would be getting ready for work. Though he was single he had a good job and couldn't be late or he could be fired. He'd already been late two times that week due to his Uncle William's demands.

"Unc, get it yourself!" Bob growled as he put on his shoes. "I'm late for work."

"Bob, I hurt my arm and can't get coffee. Please get in here and look at me."

Bob sighs and goes into the kitchen. He finds his Uncle standing in a pool of blood. The poor man was trying to cut a loaf of bread with a knife. It was apparent that the man's hand had slip and he'd plunged the knife into his arm up to the hilt.

Bob, of course, was horrified and immediately phoned the ambulance. When, a week later, Uncle William came home, Bob decided that he'd had enough of looking after him. With no other relatives around and no one else he could trust, he phoned the local Nursing home and told them that a man that was dependent on him was now too much to handle. Just like Carm, Uncle William was taken into the Nursing Home by Bob this time. He was told he was there only for observation and would be there for another week.

What is really sad is that William is, as I said, based on a true person but with a different name. That person, William I'll still call him, was placed into care by a loving daughter. William was brought into observation after a fall where he almost broke a hip. In real life, William was in his mid-70's. The poor man died in the nursing home at the age of 87. Can you imagine? Over 12 years in a nursing home and all you want to do is go back to your real home? That is another reason why the law needs to be changed. It should read something like: "If a patient at a Nursing Home is competent enough to object to their presence in that specific institution; if they can name the name of their Doctor or Psychiatrist and remember their date of birth, there is NO REASON to keep them in that institution forever. Instead, they should be given a mental health examination and if found mentally competent by a Tribunal which should include their peers but NOT their next of kin who 'incarcerated' them, then they should be released IMMEDIATELY. Moreover, the local government must give that released person aid and comfort in the form of independent housing with a caregiver who will help them to return to a community of their choice."

I'm not a Congressman or a Lawyer. But a new law specifically about nursing homes and their patients' needs to be written and passed by legislatures throughout the world. Like the new Mental Health Act 2001 in Ireland, nursing home patients MUST HAVE LEGAL RIGHTS.

As of now – they do not. Sadly, I suspect that they never will. No one pays attention to Nursing Home patients. Which is another reason why we're here:

To give the Silent a BIG VOICE!

Guideline Number 3

Learn to Take Care of Yourself FIRST

> Guideline Number 3
> … you MUST do that. When you do, you can then help your loving spouse, partner or friend with any illness, problem or issue at all.

As a Typical A Type, long ago I put others first rather than me first. This had a great deal to do with how I was raised and the many places we lived during my Dad's Airline Career. I've often been asked how many houses I've lived in since I was only an infant. The answer is more than 25 and, when Carm and I moved down to Eyeries, I knew that this would be the last move that either of us would make.

But I was wrong yet again. Carm's moved into that Nursing Home 7 hours north northwest of west by car from our Eyeries home. Right now, there's not much I can do about this situation and I know that now. Though I don't like it at all! But slowly, I've learned to live with it. Kind of...

Here's what I've learned about myself, Tom Richards, and how I use my new knowledge to stay strong, courageous, independent, disciplined and active all the time.

- I've learned to say NO – when I have to. I used to say 'Yes' all the time even when I didn't have time to help those that asked me. NO is the best word and action I've learned so far.

- Stay Active! – I have a tendency to think about Carm all the time. I wonder each morning and many times a day 'What's my little Pookey doing right now in that nursing home? Is she having breakfast? Taking a shower or a bath? Is she watching a Soap on TV like Coronation Street? Is she doing some exercises or having a cup of tea with one of the residents and their nurse? When she goes to bed and says her prayers like she always does, will Carm remember to include Tom, too? But these thoughts, while not harmful, do me no real good. When I'm active many other toxic questions disappear from my head. So what do I do to stay active?

- Because I had a Heart Attack over 2 years ago, the Surgeon recommended a great deal of exercise. So I try to do something every day to keep me fit. I lift weights, practice Yoga, Garden, walk, play Golf when the weather permits, Snorkel at the nearby beach when the water isn't too cold. Take care of our many tent campers (we having a camping site in back of our home). Feed our two pets, Sasha our cat and Bluebell our new Puppy. Occasionally I'll fly a light aircraft. I'll build model airplanes like I did when I was a kid. I read all the time. I play piano just like I played for Carm (I find this very painful to do. Carm would listen to me play and when I finally had some music right, she'd get up and Applaud for me!) Now, and because I bought a sailboat, every week I go sailing when the wind is right and there are no storms or gales forecast.

- These activities seem to cleanse my system. I focus on them (just like I'm focusing on what I'm typing now to you) and for a few minutes or an hour or even more, I'll forget all of the issues and problems that are bothering me. And yet – Carm is always at the back of my head as if she's playing Golf with me or sailing with me, or just enjoying each other's company as we always used to.

- Counselling – every few weeks I go to a wonderful counsellor not far from where I live. We actually 'role play' and I use little plastic model dinosaurs to play those that I love and those that I don't love who have harmed Carm and me. That few minutes really helps. Sometimes I became so angry that I'd go outside and yell until my anger disappeared. Or I'd throw rocks as hard as I could into the nearby Sea. Nothing really worked to dissolve my anger toward the people that had hurt me and Carm. But counselling – that truly helps. For instance, last week my counsellor, call her J here, told me that Grief needs rituals. Such as a burial when people die. So what I did today was: I found a small ring box that Carm used to use. I put in 3 earrings, unmatching. I found a large Plastic bag that seals. To that bag I added the ring box, a letter to Carm from me that's full of hope and love for our future, and 3 pictures of Carmel Murray taken right before I met her. She's perhaps 35 years old and she is absolutely beautiful! Wow, am I so glad I met her and that we lived together. I sealed the envelope, wrapped it in Tin Foil, and buried it near our beloved Tabby Cat who died by my side, as well as Carm's five years ago. Someday, I'll dig up that Plastic 'envelope' and see what's inside. It' full of loving memories: of Carm, of me and of me and Carm. What a treasure! J was right. The Ritual of a burial has helped at least somewhat.

1.

I use many other activities to get through the day - making dinner is one of them. Frankly, I hate eating alone. When Carm first disappeared from my life, I hardly ate at all. I had no appetite. All I did was sob and cry and get Angry at my God. All I wanted is for Carm to return to me. Then, over two years ago, I didn't realise that it wasn't in her power to come home. I do now and at times, because of being denied access to her, I still CAN'T STAND IT!

Now, a little bit about what I saw in Carmel. When I first met Carm, in 2009, her mental and physical health was absolutely perfect. Yes, she limped a bit due to those Cancer Treatments. But she talked well (Carm now has Aphasia, just like Bruce Willis and has trouble talking), thought better than me, was emotionally stronger than me and believed in a God above that would solve every problem that she prayed daily about.

After she moved here to Eyeries, I began to notice a few things. This started happening about four years ago.

Carm's limp became more pronounced. Sometimes, she would fall and, if I wasn't with her, would skin her knees, tear her trousers, and sometimes hurt both of her wrists. That imbalance became more pronounced. Our home has a 'sunken back dining room' that Carm named the View Room because of the stunning views of the Bay about a half mile from our back window. Two steps go down from the Living

Room to the View Room. Carm would walk out to be with me and fall down those two steps, right on her face. I'd pick her up and sometimes, she would have bruised her cheeks and forehead and on one occasion bloodied her nose. I asked Carm if we should go to our Doctor, but Carm always laughed it off and told me the imbalance was due to new medications she was taking.

Then I noticed that she couldn't pronounce certain words anymore. "Tom, can you please take out the garbage" became "Thom, can yee plssss tase out the garb." Words like that. It was as if she was suddenly lisping or just slurring her words. Frankly, I didn't think much of that small issue. I thought Carm might simply have been tired when that happened and it didn't happen often. Nor did I worry when she began to forget people's names and had to ask them again. She started to mix up even friend's names. So Yvonne became Joss. And Tom became Geoff. Or Jesu would become Hebrew. Things like that. Again, I wasn't worried (I should have been at that point) because I often mix up or forget names. That happens to almost everyone!

A few months before Carm was Stolen from me, I started to see things her that finally made me worry. Carm and I liked to play Cards together. We did that all the time when she moved here. We'd sit at our dining room table, take out a deck of cards and put all the coins that we had in our pocket on the table. We played Gin Rummy. The bet to start was always a Penny. We also played Poker. The bet to start was always 50 cents.

Carm always beat me! She was so good at playing cards and she was Brilliant even as a young woman. She'd beat all of her sisters as well as her mother and father. She'd put all of the coins in a glass jar and that would be enough for glass of beer to three.

Oh, how we laughed when she'd beat me. Occasionally, because she felt sorry for me, she'd let me win. I'd look at her and smile. "You let me win that hand, didn't you, Pook?" I'd ask. She'd laugh and say, "Yes, and never again!"

One evening, we decided to play cards again. It had been awhile since we'd taken out the card deck. It was my turn to shuffle and, as I remember, we were playing Gin Rummy. This time I was determined to beat Carm out of every penny she had! So I shuffled and gave her seven cards. She picked them up and studied them like she always did. Then she looked at me with a frown on her face.

"Tom, what card is that? It's an Ace of Hearts, isn't it?"

I took the card and looked. "No, Carm, that's a Jack of Spades. See?"

I gave her the card and she looked hard at it. "That's not Spades. That's Hearts!"

I could see the frustration in her eyes. She studied another card in her hand. "And that's a Joker, isn't it?" She showed it to me. It was an 8 of Diamonds. I sat back in my chair and looked at my poor wife and partner. She looked at me and knew she was wrong again. Now angry with herself (not me) she picked up the entire deck and threw them into the air, so hard that they hit the ceiling. She turned around and stormed back into the living room.

As I picked the cards up from the floor, I remember the soft crying that came from the living room. When I walked back in, I sat by her and took her hand.

"Tom, what's wrong with me? What the hell is wrong?" she whimpered as she kept crying.

"Nothing," I said, taking her hand. "Don't worry, Carm. If this really means something, this confusion, we'll go to the doctor. Maybe it's your vision?"

I knew her confusion with the cards had nothing to do with her vision. Then we turned the lights and television off, brushed our teeth and went to bed.

A few days later, she was gone from my sight. But I'd see her again in 7 weeks.

Such is dementia and Alzheimer's. I had no idea what was wrong with my darling girl. When she left our home, I started doing intensive research on all of her symptoms. At first, I thought she might have a brain tumour. Then, I thought it was PTSD. Then, I was certain she had Alzheimer's.

But as I've written, I was wrong once again.

By following this Third Guideline, I've becoming stronger and more aware of myself and what I really NEED. I need to eat. I need to sleep (I couldn't sleep for months after Carm left). I NEED to exercise and share with people who understand me and can relate to my personal situation. I need to relax sometimes and I've learned to do nothing at all except to Meditate. I've learned to stop beating myself up for all of the mistakes I've made. I've started to Pray again, many times each day: for Carmel and our families. For our mutual strength and love. Daily I pray one thing: that God will make some miracles – that soon, Carm will come home to me and be more perfect than when I last saw her.

If you're in a similar situation, and many are, then I pray each day for you and your partner, too. God bless You. Amen.

Guideline Number 4

Find and Retain a Good Lawyer: You May Need One

> Guideline Number 4
>
> <u>In the US, you'll need a good lawyer.</u> In Europe, under the Torte system of Justice, you'll need a good solicitor and will also have to retain a Barrister at some point. If relevant to your situation, do that as soon as you can

Carmel Murray literally disappeared from Eyeries Village, County Cork on October 8, 2021. I searched everywhere for her. I thought she may have taken our dog Jack, a Bizon Frieze, for a walk down to a Dog Grooming and Kennel business only one-half mile away. Upset because I couldn't find her, I considered phoning the Gards (Police) Station in Bantry but I decided not to. The problem was that Carm and I never left the house unexpectedly without telling each other.

Upset and not sure what to do, I climbed into our blue Mitsubishi Pickup Truck and drove down to see if I could find Carm and Jack. When I arrived at the Kennel facility, I found the owner, a friend of ours, and asked if she saw Carm. This very nice woman nodded her head.

"Tom, Carm came down here with Jack about an hour ago. She was dragging a small piece of luggage behind her. Jack was on his lead and the only thing that Carm was carrying was her large bag. When she arrived here, I was inside cutting the hair of a dog. But I heard a car horn honk and, thinking it was a customer, went outside. There, I saw a dark grey car come down the hill into our small parking lot. The woman behind the wheel looked vaguely familiar. Carm opened the back door, put Jack and her luggage in, then climbed into the passenger seat. I waved at Carm but she ignored me which she never does. The car drove off quickly.

I thanked the woman and drove back to our home. There, I sat down and held my mobile phone in my hand. I decided to call my partner and when I did, all I heard was Carm's voicemail. "Leave a message, please." So I did. I asked her where she was and why she didn't tell me where she was going. A few minutes later, I decided to take the Pickup around the area to see if I could spot the grey car with Carmel and someone else inside. When I climbed into my pickup, I found a plastic bag on the floor at the passenger's side. In it, I discovered all of Carm's expensive jewelry: her engagement ring, the ring I had bought her in Boston, rings I had given to her over the years that were quite valuable; the golden necklace that Dad had given to Carm when my Mom died and all sorts of other necklaces that Dad had given to her; all of the jewelry that her mother had left her. And at the bottom were a few coins and Jack's water and food dishes.

I picked up the bag and walked back into the house. Locking the front door behind me, I stood in the middle of the kitchen and began crying. I honestly thought that Carm had broken up with me. She'd returned all the expensive jewelry that Dad, I and her mother had given to her over the years. What I couldn't understand is why she didn't take some of it. Like the jewelry that her mother bequeathed her when Josephine finally passed away.

Confused? Yes I was confused. Confused, upset, indecisive, unprepared for this surprising event. I didn't know what to do!

I do now of course. But before I write why I made the decision to find a good legal firm, let me tell you one more small story about Carm. Maybe two.

For three days I didn't hear a word from Carm. On the fourth day my mobile phone rang and on it was Carm! I couldn't believe my ears. I realised, at that point, that she was alive. But I didn't know where she was. She told me that she was in the Trim area, staying with a sister, Mars. Mars had brought her to her house and she was going to stay a few days. Carm promised me that she'd call back later that day or the next morning.

She did phone back the next morning. And the next and the next. Eventually, she told me she was ready to come home. So I packed as quick as I could and drove up to the Trim area to pick her up as well as Jack. When I came to Mars's house, Carm was at the open front window. I walked quickly toward her, absolutely delighted to see her.

"Carm, you're okay, aren't you," I said. "Why don't you come outside and I'll take you and Jack home."

Carm didn't reply. Instead, her eyes held a type of hatred that I'd never seen before. I reached up through the open window, and on tiptoes, touched her check. She slapped my hand away and said something like: "Don't you ever, ever touch me again. You bastard!" She turned and walked away. I was so upset again but there was nothing that I could do. I was powerless. That day, I drove back to Eyeries (a 7-hour drive) and waited for Carm to call again.

Two days after I came home, Carm rang. This time she sounded like the 'normal' Carm. We talked for over a half-hour. She seemed somewhat upset and I asked her what was wrong.

"Jack is quite sick again," Carm said. "He won't eat and is becoming incontinent so he won't drink either."

"Oh, God, NO!" I replied. Let me explain: because Carm couldn't have children Jack was like her son - her only child. She had purchased Jack when he was only a few months old, flying him from Kansas City to Boston. She'd had him ever since, and when she made the decision to come back to Ireland, her company paid the airfare and all of the related expenses to have Jack flown back, too. Carm would never ever have left Jack in the States. She loved that dog as much as she loved me. Carm promised she'd keep in touch about Jack's condition. That night, at 10PM, I was in bed sleeping. I'd been dreaming deeply but my phone rang beside me. Getting up, I answered the phone and heard Carm on the phone in tears.

"Our son Jack is gone to heaven," Carm said. "He didn't suffer at all. I took him to the local Vet and she inserted the needle. Jack held out his paw to me, like he always did for both of us. I took it, he growled a little and seemed to smile. Then he closed his eyes and went to sleep."

She said much more about Jack going to heaven. What's frankly amazing is this: the dream I had was exactly like what Carm told me. At exactly the time that Jack had taken his last breathe, I dreamed that our little dog of fifteen years had finally gone to 'Doggie Heaven' as Carm called it. Carm and I were so close that sometimes, we even dreamed what each other had done that day in reality. That's how close we were. It was as if we shared the same soul at times.

After Jack died, Carm made the decision to come back to our home. She had called me and when she said that she was coming home, she handed her mobile phone to Mars. Mars said that Carm was coming back but only for a visit. Carm took the phone back and said she was coming home permanently. Which is what she did. I picked her up at the Killarney Train Station. It was as if Carm was normal again. Completely normal! We took a walk around that large town and she had her hair done. I waited in the lobby for her and when she was done, I paid the hairdresser. She looked not only healthy but absolutely heavenly again. I took her arm and we went to a nearby restaurant for lunch. Then we walked to a phone shop (Vodafone) to have her phone fixed. After that, I drove us home (Carm never did learn how to drive on the narrow rural roads near our home so she let me do all the driving). Halfway to a town called Kenmare, I pulled into a lovely Forested

Park where we always walked Jack. I got out and went to the other side of the car. Carm opened her door and I smiled at her.

"Carm, I'm now certain that I'll be divorced within months. It's time to seal the deal on the promises we made to each other." I pulled out a ring box and got down on my knees and for the hundredth time asked her to marry me. She opened the box to find an eternity ring inside made by a local Kenmare jeweler. Putting it on her thin ring finger, she climbed out of the car and hugged me. "Yes. A thousand times yes," she said, tears in her eyes. We climbed back in the car and drove home.

Carm and I were supposed to finally get married at Easter, 2022. But, as you know, things happened. She and I have been legally engaged since 2009 but 'engagement' means nothing in the law. It has no legal definition. Sometimes, one of Carm's relatives will say to me (usually in a letter): "Tom Richards never loved Carm at all. Tom was a cruel, unkind, bossy man who never let Carmel come up to visit us in County Meath. Tom locked her in their outdoor shed then beat the crap out of her."

Today, all I can do is sigh. Lies, every one of them. Or a whole lot of confusion about the difference between me at Carmel Murray's former husband, George. In the next Chapter, I'll describe the nature of that confusion.

Carm stayed for five nights. Each morning she'd be the same loving Carm that I'd always known. But at 2PM each day (it was mid-January) as the sun started to go down, she'd change. She had Sundowners Syndrome.

I'd seen the same thing in my Dad right before he passed away. Carm became Jekyll and Hyde. In the morning she was wonderful. After 2PM she became depressed, angry and kept threatening to leave her again if I, and I quote, "Wouldn't stop annoying her." So I gave her a great deal of space and considered once again phoning our doctor.

On the fifth day of her stay, it was a Sunday afternoon, I went up to our local pub, Causkey's Bar, like we usually did on most Sunday's before dinner. I had spaghetti on and Carm told me to go up to Causkeys while she was getting dressed.

At the Bar, I ordered two bottles of Heineken from the owner, Mrs C. As I was sipping my bottle of beer, the front door CRASHED open. And I mean CRASHED. Carm had pushed the door open so hard it almost broke the door's window. Storming in, she pointed her finger at me and this is what she said. Her exact words.

"George, keep your hands off me! Don't ever touch me again! The next time you try to hit me, I'll sick that Gards on you! You bastard! You cunt! You unforgivable monster man!"

I looked at Mrs C and she looked back at me and then to Carm.

"Carmel, why don't you sit down at the bar and I'll make you a cup of tea." Carm sat down, absolutely fuming. He wouldn't look at me. When the tea was ready, Mrs C carried it out and sat across the bar from Carm. Though Mrs C tried to talk to Carmel, Carm wouldn't even look at her either. Her voice was silent and I gather it still is.

Finishing her tea, Carm got up and finally looked me in the eye. "I'm sorry, Tom," she said. "I think I'll have a nap." She left the Bar and when she was gone I picked up my phone and called Mars. I told Mars that I knew the time had come for Carmel to go to hospital to examine her. I told her that after I finished that brief call, I was going to phone our Ambulance Service. Mars agreed with every word I said. So I phoned that Service and a few minutes later they were there.

I met them just outside of Causkeys and talked to the driver. He told me to stay in the Bar. "Tom, when you phoned you told us how angry your partner was. The best thing for you to do is stay here. We'll pick up Carm and get her to Bantry Hospital. Then you can come visit her."

Later, I was told by a woman at the Ambulance Service that when they picked Carm up, my little Pookey was standing on the stairs with a hard case pink suitcase. I know that one so well too. She said to both EMT's. "Hi and thanks for picking me up. I guess it's time I went into hospital for a day or two."

They put her into the Ambulance and drove her away. And here's one of the Biggest mistakes – call it a complete Failure – that I made. I should have followed that ambulance and when we got to the hospital, taken Carm inside. Covid had essentially closed the hospital to visitors. But when I'd seen a nurse or doctor, as Carmel was checked in, I would have told them that I was Carm's Next-of-Kin.

That's all I had to do! But did I! No again.

This Chapter is about the Law and getting a lawyer. That's why, when I finally realized my mistake I tried to hire a good law firm as soon as I could. The problem? They were all too busy. (NOTE: Mars had Promised me months ago that if and when Carm went into any hospital, we would be joint Next of Kin's. That didn't happen. That person broke her promise to me many times as did all of Carm's relatives and her best friend.)

After the ambulance took her into hospital in Bantry (about an hour's drive) I visited one time. I took a brand-new Nokia phone with me (I bought it at my local 3 dealership and asked the owner to give her a new phone number because Carm had accidentally left her Old phone in our home and I tried to charge it but discovered I couldn't). When I walked into the Hospital Reception Room, I found a nurse and explained our situation. "Nurse, can you please give this brand-new phone to Carm. See?" I said talking it out of its box. "I charged it and it has a new phone number. I've placed my number in that phone as well as the numbers of relatives and friends. When she's feeling a bit better, would you ask her to phone me?"

The Nurse took the phone from me as well as the box She told me she'd give it to Carm as soon as she saw her that afternoon.

Now, here's another real crime! A month later, have received no phone call from Carm, I was able to charge her old phone. When I opened it, I found all of her applications on the Home Screen. I opened one of them, WhatsApp, and found a group called THE RELATIVES. I instantly opened it. What I discovered made me what to either laugh or cry.

It turned out that when Carm had disappeared from our Village... remember that a dark grey saloon car had picked her and Jack up? A message popped up saying to all of the members of the Group: "Hi all! It's Alpha here. I'm delighted to tell you that Carm is safe. I picked her up at a Groomer's as well as Jack and our sister's luggage. I drove her up to Mars's home. More later. Alpha."

I could NOT believe it! Alpha had been to visit us a few months before when I was with my Dad in Florida. But at least now I knew what really happened. Carm truly had been stolen from me!

The second message I came across on THE RELATIVES GROUP was a short message and a picture from Mars. It said, "All, Tom will never be able to talk to Carmel again. See? My son and I smashed the phone that that hurtful man had given to her. Halleluia! Mars and (name of son). The picture showed Carmel's new phone, still in its box, on a tile floor. The box was torn and pieces of that brand new Nokia phone were scattered on tiles across the large phone. Mars and her son were looking down at those many pieces and both were LAUGHING!

Again, I couldn't believe my eyes. Mars had come down a few years ago with her new Partner. Carm and I really liked the New Partner and we drove them both all over the Beara Peninsula. We let them sleep in our home, of course, and the Partner and I became great friends (unfortunately, that new Partner had a massive heart attack and died only a few months after I first met him).

These two mysteries had finally been solved. But now what should I do? I phoned the hospital a number of times and the only answer I received from them was, "Sorry, Carmel Murray is no longer here." I started worrying that Carm had either escaped from that hospital and was wandering around Bantry in the rain. She could have easily been hit by a car or a bus. Deciding to finally take some sort of Action, I created a small Missing Person's poster and taped it to windows around our village. I took a poster to our Local Garda Station and, driving up to Bantry again, visited the Garda Station. There, I met a wonderful female Garda. I was brought into a back room and as I dictated, she took down the Official Missing Person's Report. I had a photo of Carmel in my wallet and gave that to her. She took it and said, "Mister Richards, I'll upload my written report and this photo into our central database. All the Garda in Ireland will start to look for her."

Then she peered closely at the picture. "I know this woman, don't I? Isn't she in Bantry hospital?"

"No Ma'am," I replied and explained that I had phoned a number of times but was told Carm was not in the hospital anymore.

"Wait right here while I make a call," the kind Garda stated. When she came back a few minutes later she smiled and said, "Tom, Carm's still in the Bantry Hospital. I'm sorry, but you can't see her. She has Covid right now and so the hospital has been locked down to all visitors."

I can't describe the relief that I felt at that moment! Carm's not dead? And I can't see her but then no one can see their friends or relatives due to Covid. I went home feeling much lighter than I had in months!

But more months passed and still no word about Carm. I phoned the hospital a number of times but no response from a nurse or a doctor. Finally, I got through to one of Carm's nurses. She told me, "Mister Richards, I'm sorry but you're not her Next of Kin. I'm afraid I can't tell you anything at all about Carm or her condition."

I hung up and it was then and there that I decided to take REAL action.

For the next three months, I emailed every national politician I could find on the Dail List (the Dail is sort of like the House of Representatives). I kept a spreadsheet, and when I had finished I had emailed well over 200 national representatives (called TD's here in Ireland). I also emailed the then Taoiseach (very much like the Prime Minster of the UK). I did receive back 5 responses. All of those emails, usually sent by their Personal Assistance, said that they could do nothing to help me. I emailed (and phoned) the US Embassy. Carm, if you'll remember, is a U.S. citizen and I was sure that they would help. A very kind woman, an official in the U.S. Embassy in Dublin, apologises but said that because Carm was being held in Ireland there was absolutely nothing they could do. There hands were tied. Furthermore, she explained that if Carm and I were in the United States, they would work very hard to ensure that I could visit Carm as much as they wanted.

On and on it went and no success at all. I met with a TD in Bantry (one of my local national representatives) and he told me he would help. I was so overjoyed by his answer that after our meeting was over, I went out onto the street and started Bawling. This TD told me he would contact the HSE (our Health Authority) and begin the process to get me access. Months passed and when I finally contacted him again, his kind, intelligent TD told me, "Tom, they're giving me the run-around again. The HSE state that they are not responsible for anyone like Carmel while she's in hospital, even though Carm is in a publicly funded hospital. They say they can help only when she's put in a government funded nursing home but that could be a full year from now."

I thanked that man, hung up and burst into tears. Once again I was without hope.

This is what happens if you're in my situation. Promises are made then broken. Government officials can't really help you. You're trapped in a prison not of your own making but of Carm's dim-witted Relatives.

Months again passed. I was literally without hope and had become depressed. Two events happened that changed my life. First, I truly considered suicide. My plans were these: 1. I could easily hang myself in the backyard shed. No one would find me for weeks! What I wonderful way to go, I thought to myself as I learned how to tie a hangman's noose. Or, if I wasn't brave enough to do that, 2. Because I fly general aviation aircraft - light planes - I could drive up to Faranfore and visit Kerry Airport. I knew there were many lightplanes there. Often, pilot's don't need a key to start them, or the key to almost any plane is kept in an unlocked box in the airport hangar. The plan was so easy! I'd go up early in the morning, take the key when no one was looking, start any aircraft that I could find, taxi out to the Active Runway without the radio on and, before the Control Tower could object, take off! Then I'd head straight west. I'd fly for as long as I had fuel, at a very low level so that no radar could spot me. Then I'd do a few aerobatics and, when the fuel indicator was at Zero, I'd point her nose at the sea, say my prayers and - SPLASH! - Dead.

Of course I took none of those actions. Which is why I'm able to type this. The second big event was when I had my Heart Attack. That truly changed my life. I realized that I did have reason to live. If I died, no one would be here to take care of Carmel, my loving soulmate. Having survived from this almost fatal accident, I phoned a great lawyer in Bantry, not far from where Carm was. His name is Ray and I'm sure he won't mind me using his real first name (there are many lawyers and solicitors in Ireland with the first name Ray). I told Ray and his legal assistant, Mike, what had happened to me and Carm. Both men were absolutely appalled! They told me about the new Decision-Making Act that was going through various committees in the Dail and stated that soon, I would be made Carm's sole Decisionmaker

Once again I had reason to hope! It was then that I changed my will to make certain that if I passed away, Carm would have enough money and assets to live comfortably for the rest of her life! Ray charged me exactly €100 in cash to help me change the Will.

Ray retired a few months ago. Now I have a law firm working for me. The senior partner's name is P. Little. A giant of a man, he has told me that I have every right to see Carm. The two of them met years ago and Carm told me then that with Mister Little in my corner, I would never lose any legal action at all. Little and I hired a Barrister and that good woman's opinion is this: of course I can see Carm. All I need is a Court Order. Courts are closed in Ireland throughout the month of August so I'm hoping that I can see Carmel Murry by my birthday, 4 October 2024. That's not far at all! The Barrister charged my only €950 for her legal opinion. So as of this date, in August 2024, I've spent a total of €1050 on those two legal bills. Of course that doesn't count Carm's new Nokia phone (€1540), the various gifts and personal belongings that I've delivered to her or sent to her (she may never receive them because that Nursing Home and her Next of Kin does not want Carm to be reminded at all of Tom Richards), nor does it include Travel up and down to at least Try to see her, phone bills and similar. It's a small price to pay, anyway, to try to gain access to my Almost-wife.

In the next chapter, I'm going to cover the next Guideline: Do Your Research. And that starts with finding out from various friends that know Carm very well, where she actually is. Once again, Get this:

Without my knowledge, Carm's relatives (her Next of Kin) made the decision to move Carm to that Nursing Home north of me. I happened to drive into Trim about 2 years ago on the way to visit my children and grandchildren. Along the way, I stopped at the local cemetery to pay my respects to Tommy and Josephine Murray, who are buried there. As I was walking toward that Family Plot, I saw a woman about my age walking toward me. Looking up, she then recognised me. I'll call her Mrs O'C.

"Tom Richards, it's been an age since I've seen you!" she exclaimed. "How are you?"

"Mrs O'C, I'm not good. You heard about Carm, didn't you?"

"Of course I did. My home is right down the street from Carm's parents old home. But why are you so upset? Haven't you heard the good news?"

"News?" I asked. "What news."

"My daughter works for the Nursing home where Josephine was a resident until a few days before she passed away. My daughter, who still works there, told me that Carmel Murray had been moved in a few days back. She's now a resident. That means when you're up here, you can visit her anytime you want. You visited Josephine, didn't you? She treated you like her son. She never had a son and always wanted one."

"I know she did. I really miss her, Mrs O'C as well as Tommy. But, well, I've been told that I can't visit Carm at any time."

"What nonsense!" she said in reply. "Then hire a good lawyer and you'll both be fine."

"I will Mrs O'C. Thank you and your daughter for the information."

It had started to rain so that kind woman hurried to her car parked right outside the Cemetery.

See? Some people are very, very kind when they find out about your situation. They'll even give you advice based on their own experiences. But others? They can be not so kind or, frankly, they don't give a good Damn.

As I end this chapter my head hurts. I look out the window at the fog that hugs our coastline. I look at Carm's picture, shake my head and smile.

"Carmel, darling, this world of ours has gone stark raving mad!"

Guideline Number 5

Conduct Exhaustive Research

> Guideline Number 5
>
> ... and by EXHAUSTIVE, I mean it! – on Dementia, Alzheimer's and similar mental diseases. Lawyers, Barristers, Solicitors. Local and national Politicians. Influencers like Psychiatrists and Directors of Nursing. Friends and relatives that can DEMONSTRATE the length of your relationship and how you loved each other. And this is just SOME of the research.

As I've written, I am NOT a professional lawyer, doctor, psychiatrist, therapist or psychologist. But that did not stop me from conducting extensive RELEVANT research across a number of disciplines. Everything from the law regarding Mental Health Issues, to new medications and therapies to help stop and reverse Memory Loss; finding all of the politicians and specialists I should contact to help me gain IMMEDIATE access to Carm; signs and symptoms of Alzheimer's and Dementia, specific research on Ireland's Mental Health Acts 2001 - 2018 and how they might help me FORCE a professional diagnosis of Carmel's many memory and behavioural symptoms; backgrounds on Carm's family history as well as my own to show the long-term relationships of our two families; locating Carmel Murray's medical forms and medical histories going back at least 20 or more years; conducting extensive Research regarding the history of

George and his family and how that will help me to access Carm; research (and courses) on how to take care of Alzheimer's and Dementia patients (how to communicate with them in a Memory Book, what to say – or not say – when I finally get to see her); COMPREHENSIVE Research on the latest medications and therapies now available in the United States and all of Europe (including Ireland); on-going research with Legal Professional regarding our new Mental Health Law, the Decision-Making Act 2015 to Present (that new law is constantly changing as Judges interpret various aspects of that new law during Court Hearings to determine a Patient's legal Decisionmaker.

For obvious reason, I won't go into detail. I'll only bullet point some of my findings.

- Carmel Murray's family and my family are related through Ancestry: from the moment I met Carm on that magical flight from Boston to Dublin, I knew in my heart that for reasons I wouldn't understand for many, many years, Carm and I were related by blood. It turns out that my feelings were true (Carm felt the same way about me). Carm's mother, Josephine, was French by blood. Her ancestors travelled from France to Prince Edward Island, Canada, in the 1700's. There, they settled and established a series of Townships. In the 1800s, my ancestors also from France, sailed to Prince Edward Island and settled in Tignish, Prince Edward Island, Canada, only a hundred miles or so from that mid-PEI Township. There, both families intermarried. This was a discovery that gave me great joy. Is it any wonder that Carm and I fell in love at first sight?

- International Laws on Legal Guardianship, Legal Decisionmakers, Legal Partners, What Constitutes 'Marriage' in the Eyes of the Law – laws concerning these vital issues vary significantly across the world. All I'll write here is that many countries keep changing these laws. In Ireland, the terms "Common Law Husband" and "Common Law Wife" have very DIFFERENT interpretations depending on which Legal Professional you talk to. Some say it has no relevance to a relationship at all. Others say that these terms mean: "If (depending on the country of residence) two partners have lived together continuously for 5 or 7 years, that couple has the same legal rights as a legally married couple."

For over two years I depended on this interpretation, thinking that I would have 'legal custody' of Carmel immediately. The problem? In Ireland, as it turns out, this is NOT THE LAW. In some countries IT IS THE LAW. As Carm's common law husband, all I can do is change my will (which I've done) to provide for her. Common Law spouses have other legal rights. If you are living in Ireland and read this, hire a Solicitor and Barrister to gain access to your Spouse. If you live in other countries, check with your lawyer. You may have legal rights to become your Spouses' Legal Guardian immediately. The other legal term that infuriates me, at least in Ireland, is 'Next of Kin'. That term is a convenience for the medical profession and is not recognised as Law. At least not in Ireland. My research of that term indicated to me that the term also has little meaning in laws across the world. This means that, technically, those that use 'Next of Kin' as a reason to deny you and me access to your family / friend suffering from Dementia, Alzheimer's oar other serious illnesses are stretching the truth. Again, consult a legal professional if you're being denied access.

- Medications / Therapies for Dementia and Alzheimer's Sufferers – I started to do research in this area when Carm was first taken into Hospital. Pharmaceutical companies, most in the U.S., continue to invest in research. In Ireland, to my knowledge only THREE (count them: 3!) memory loss medications have been approved for use in these patients. Which, it seems to me, is unpardonable! The Alzheimer's Association (U.S.) lists a number of medications that can slow, stop or even halt a Patient's decline in Memory. See https://www.alz.org/alzheimers-dementia/treatments/medications-for-memory for the complete list. These include Aducanumab, Donanemab and Lecanemab. I have also been told by a number of Azheimer's and Dementia professionals that T-Cell Therapy has recently been approved in the US by the FDA. While this therapy is still undergoing extensive testing, Patients (with an agreement by their family members) can use this therapy to reverse memory loss. This is, of course, an astounding scientific breakthrough. Research states that over the next ten years, T-Cell therapy will become relatively common to treat Patients across the world. Scientists are hoping that one day, T-

Cell therapy, used with drug therapy, will PREVENT these terrible Illnesses.

- Research Alzheimer's and Dementia Diseases – the key to helping your relatives (or legal teams) to understand the above diseases is to do some basic research. All I wanted to learn is what caused Memory Loss in human beings, with special emphasis on someone as young as Carm. I can now conduct conversations, basic ones, with psychiatrists and doctors who are experts in these areas. (What truly astounded me as I conducted this research is that people in their mid-30's can suffer from Early Onset Alzheimer's. When I found this, I was so sad. I thought that Carm would die by the time she was 64 years old. At that point, I had no hope that I would ever see her again, except to leave flowers beside her grave). Please conduct this basic research. You can find books and information either online, in a local hospital or often in your local library. And don't be afraid to ask you family doctor about these dreadful Illnesses. They'll explain it to you with full colour pictures showing the brain as well as text and diagrams. Too, they'll put in language that a non-professional can understand.

- Conduct deep research on your legal teams – this is a mistake that I made for a long, long time. I quickly learned which legal teams were not interested in helping me either because a) they were too busy; b) they were focusing on a single area of the law that had nothing to do with getting me access to Carm; or c) they had no understanding of this vital area of the law and had no interest in learning it. It doesn't take much time to understand if they can help you or not. Talk to them first, then send them a very short explanation of what you need to do (getting access to your loved one, for instance). Explain what you've already tried to do. Do NOT tell them that you've been in touch with, or have worked with, another legal team. For some reason, this will bias a Legal Team that you're approaching and they may well refuse to take your case.

The above bullet points are only some of the research that I've done over the past years. I have over 100 folders in my laptop on the research that I've conducted and what I've tried to do for Carm and myself.

A last point: KEEP EVERYTHING and I mean Everything pertaining to your hunt for justice regarding your Spouse, family member or friend. If you receive a letter from a nursing home, doctor, lawyer or psychiatrist, scan it and file it in a computer. Keep the original. If you make any notes, scan them or type them and keep them. If you receive an email that seems threatening to you or that special person you love, also save that to your computer. If you have old letters and pictures that show the loving relationship that you had (and still have) keep the originals in a safe place. If you have old receipts, joint bank account statements with both your names on them; old or current passports and driver's licenses used by that special person; save them. Save EVERYTHING. Your lawyer will someday thank you and this will help you gain access quickly.

Guideline Number 6

Bad Things Happen to Good People...

> Guideline Number 6
>
> ... ALL THE TIME! Do your very best to get over that horrible reality. For years, I couldn't. For all sorts of reasons, it prevented me from taking ACTION.

This will be a very short chapter and based on my personal experiences and the experiences of those that I've talked to or read about.

Question: Why? Why did this happen to me and Carmel? Why did she, of all people, acquire this dreadful Disease so early in her life? Why did I have to go through this? I always try my best to treat people with kindness and even love. So did Carm. Why can't I help her or myself now? Answer: see below!

My parents always told me that, as I became older, I could experience unfair situations. They were right, unfortunately. But today, as with all days, I read the news and find articles that cause me great joy or unbelievable pain.

Last night was the Closing of the 2024 Olympics in Paris. And what joy I felt as I watched that huge celebration in that giant Stadium! I laughed with those that had won medals. I cried for those who had tried their best and will go home with nothing at all except the joy of participating. I pounded on the table when all of the volunteers that helped Olympic Teams and visitors were congratulated with huge Applause. I stood when the Marseilles, the French National Anthem, was played. I did so out of respect for France and all of the Athletes but also because I am significantly French. What a great time I had with my friends watching those amazing Games! Now, like many across the world, I look forward to the 2028 Olympic Games to be held in Los Angeles.

I still feel good thinking about what I saw: the people in their country's national costumes and dresses. The women from Nigeria in their huge hats. The Chinese team members - what a huge team! The Irish and US Teams that came out holding their national flags and waving them. Joy now and then is good.

But there are other times: times when I get so low in myself that I have to share with someone. In our village, we have a woman named Francis. She lost her husband at sea many years ago. He owned a large Trawler and, with a few other crew members, ventured out into the Wild Atlantic. A storm came up. The trawler was sunk. And sadly, they never found any of their bodies. They had all drowned. They held a memorial service but there were no caskets. No real funeral. Just the local people coming into our Church and praying.

I've told Francis all about Carm and I ask her advice about trying to get over this huge loss. You see, to me it seems exactly like what Francis is experiencing and has experienced for all these years. Often, it seems that Carm went to sea on a boat without me. She hit a storm. The boat capsized and Carm was stolen by the sea. I wish I could have swum out and rescue her but I didn't know that a storm was coming over the Eastern Horizon. I could have at least tried, couldn't I? When I told Francis how I felt this is what she said: "Tom, Carm is lost to the sea. She's nowhere to be found. You'll never get over her but you can always say a prayer to remember her. Loss that you're going through feels like acid has been poured into your heart. It's so unfair but it seems to me that God has willed it so.

"Francis, how can you say that? God wouldn't will my partner, my wife, to be dead."

"It's simply a matter of fate, Tom," she replied. "If Carm had not been lost to this terrible sea that you're both going through, then you wouldn't have found the strength to find her again, would you?"

I considered what she said to me and it's true. If Carm hadn't been stolen from me, I would never have experienced the depths of sorrow, sadness, and yes, joy that I have for the past three years. I wish it weren't so. I wish I could turn the clock back to 'zero' and re-experience all the love that we had for each other, all the memories, from the day we met each other until the day that she left my life.

Francis is a peach of a woman. Every time I see her in the Village she smiles at me and asks how I'm doing. I don't always tell her the truth but I always smile back.

That's a 'story' that makes me feel good too. But what about the ones that don't? From all of those stories and articles that I've read and listened to, I've learned something from them. Usually, it's this: I am NOT the only one going through the pain that I am. Simple as that.

A couple of articles that I read and I'll close this chapter. First, a number of months ago, I read about a teacher in the United States. A very healthy woman who had a husband and two children. She had a great career in a local university and then she discovered that she had cancer. Her family were horrified but they stuck right by her side.

The day she died, the family started to organise a large funeral to be attended by hundreds of this woman's friends and family. But...and here's the thing... as the husband was getting dressed for the funeral at his home, he had a fatal heart attack. The article then quoted his children. Something like, "Dad loved Mom so much that he couldn't live without her. He's now in Heaven with her and they are one again leading a wonderfully Happy life."

I finished the article and started to cry. I cried for that entire family, myself and Carm. It was as if I died again. From that single article I learned this: we are humans and the human condition means that for every life we owe a death. My faith is based on a number of believes. One of them is: if I die before Carm or if Carm dies before me, we'll meet each other in Heaven as the married couple we were fated to be. And I also believe this, which will be unbelievable to many.

Dig beneath Carm's damaged neurons and we'll still find all of her memories. The damaged memories exist in my legal Partner's tired body in that Nursing Home. The rest of her memories? The good ones? Well, you can't kill memories or your spirit. For that reason I believe that the Undamaged part of Carm's memories as well as the Strong Spirit that is truly Carmel Murray are now in some sort of Local Heaven. At night, I like to think she whispers to me. Right now, her 'ghost' is standing over my shoulder reminding me of what I should write to you. She's Alive. Right now. Just as I remember her. And if I'm very, very lucky, someday soon, perhaps by my 69th birthday, and due to the medication and treatment that she'll receive, she'll come back home better than ever before: Dementia free and cancer free. That's what I believe. I have to, you see. Or I'd again have very little hope for our future.

The last 'article' I'll tell you briefly about is a non-fiction book that I found in one of Carm's boxes. That darned book has been sitting in that book for at least ten years! I was cleaning out my office and I decided to go through that big box full of Carm's old papers and some pictures. The book was at the very bottom. I took it out, took it downstairs, and started reading it. I finished it within two days.

The book is titled: "Heaven is for Real" by Todd Burpo and a friend who is also a writer. The brief summary is: This is the story of a young boy who emerges from life-saving surgery with remarkable stories of his trip to heaven. It is the true story of Colton Burpo, the 4-year-old son of a small-town Nebraska pastor.

I had so much fun reading it! I guess Carm bought it when she lived in Boston. She read it once (there's a book marker in that short autobiography: her airplane ticket back to Ireland from Logan - I've left it in there), brought it back home to Trim, brought it here in the box and left it there. It's as if Carm has sent me a special gift. I loved that wonderful thin book! I won't go into details but here's what I learned.

Yes, there really is a Heaven. When Todd's son, Colton, goes into a local hospital with a problem that should kill him, that young boy 'dies' on the operating table. As he dies, he look down and sees his doctors struggling to bring him back to life. He also sees his parents and sisters in the Hospital. Taken immediately to Heaven, he experiences events and sees people that he'd never met before on Earth. Colton is finally saved by his surgeons, doctors and nurses. When he goes home, be begins to tell his parents what he saw and who he met. His parents, particularly his Dad Todd, can't believe what they're hearing. As one example: Colton meets his grandfather who tells him his name and sits the young boy in his lap. The grandfather died well before Colton was born. Yet the boy remembers not only the name of his Grandfather but how he looked, what he wore, how he talked and how he behaved.

By the end of this book I took away a number of points but this is the one I remember most: When Times get tough, have Faith in things you Can't SEE! Just like the faith we have in a God that we can't see. That tiny book, when I finished it, was a turning point for Tom. It made me laugh all the time, not cry. It made me have more faith in what I couldn't see and what I could see. It made me realise that my life is worth living again.

This book, Heaven is for Real! is based on fact. It's a true story and I found it to be one of the best books I've ever read. It's still available online. If you want a 'Heavenly lift!" (a really bad joke but I can't help it! Haha!) go to: https://www.awesomebooks.com/book/9780718036560/heaven-changes-everything/used?gad_source=1&gclid=Cj0KCQjw5ea1BhC6ARIsAEOG5pxlgqbiRlTV09Eg3mNhdLGzZfxcdY5FlNoRitlW1-kfEgKjKZF-BLgaAj4TEALw_wcB. That's a really long URL so, if you can't read it, Google: *Heaven is for Real* by Todd Burpo.

Sometimes, even now as I finish writing for the day, it seems that the pain in my heart and soul will go on and on and on forever. It could happen. It will stop, of course, the moment my heart stops beating. But now I know this.

My love for Carm is never ending. My love is like the Universe. It will always be there even during the day when I can't see the stars or the Moon. It is like a simple song or drumbeat. It's like a code - a semaphore - that I couldn't understand for a long time but now I do.

Have a little faith, is all I can say. Bad things happen to Good People all the time. Look at any article you'll find in the newspapers or online. Watch the news on TV or read a book based on facts. Often, you'll find that the best people in the world, those with the biggest hearts, are going through a type of misery that they can't understand (though they will) but that you recognise all too well.

And that is what life is all about. Knowing that we're never alone. In pain, joy, sorry, sickness, health and love - just like a marriage vow - life is full of splendid people with kind hearts whom you can relate to and learn something to help you cope.

Guideline Number 7

Don't Beat Yourself Up

> Guideline Number 7
>
> <u>Trying Your Very Best is all you can do.</u> In the past, when Carm was stolen, I beat myself up emotionally every day. I don't do that as often, now, but on some mornings I feel like someone is beating my head in with an axe.

Last night I had what should have been a good dream. I had been made Carm's sole Decision-Maker and, in the dream, was led into her room at that Nursing Home. When I talked to her, she looked at me and smiled. But Carm looked terrible. Her hair was unkempt, she could barely talk and though she recognised me she couldn't remember the love that we had for each other. It was as if I was talking to someone who wasn't in her right mind at all. I woke up in a sweat and, going downstairs, knew I was having an emotional hangover once again.

What's horrible is that for the past month or more my dreams about Carm (I dream about her every night) were all good dreams. In some of them, we were married. In others we were getting married. In yet others, we'd be in Florida visiting my father the way we did so many times.

Now, a dream is a dream and it isn't reality. I do know, now, that I've tried my level best to help Carm ever since she disappeared from our Village. Yet sometimes it doesn't seem to be enough. No matter how hard I've worked to contact someone who can help me access; the hours and hours I've spent writing letters and sending them out to influencers; the horrible times that I rang the Nursing Home where Carm is now staying and was told that I couldn't talk to her or visit her. All of those occasions made me beat myself up. I kept telling myself, "There's something that I'm not thinking of. Something very simple that I should be doing. Some other action I should be taking."

The Answer to myself was simple: "Tom, stop beating yourself up!"

Here's what I did to do that. But first, I'll tell you how, a few months after Carm was placed into her Nursing home, I was actually allowed to see her, not once but twice! For a total time of 20 minutes and 5 seconds. Wow! The reason I'm telling you this is to show you how, at a time that was supposed to be happy and joyous for me, I actually beat myself up emotionally not once but many times.

A month after Carm was brought to the Nursing Home in Trim, I was in a town just up the road visiting my children. When I was going through Trim on my way back to Eyeries, one of Carm's nurses phoned me on my mobile phone. She told me that I could come visit Carm - my loving partner had been asking for me. I had bought Carm a bag of new clothes and had them in our Pickup Truck. I had passed the Nursing Home so I turned around and, when I went into that lovely building, the Receptionist gave me the 4-digit code to the lockup door on the 2nd Floor. When I went upstairs in the elevator, I was met by the Nurse who had phoned me. I'll never forget the smile on that Professional's face. She led me into the day room which was full of women with Dementia and Alzheimer's. Carm was sitting at a large round table talking to one of the Residents. When she saw me, she smiled and, standing up as I walked over to her, she took my hand. I sat down beside her and, having brought my phone, showed her pictures of our Eyeries home, Jack her dog (the one that had died), a few of both of us in our home at Christmas and some of the holidays that we spent together in Portugal and in America.

When she saw the photo of Jack, she started crying almost silently and said a simple sentence to me: "Tom, there's poor Jack." She took my hand again when I gave her the bag of gifts. Just like Carm always did at Christmas and her birthday, she unwrapped all the presents and, taking them out, studied the clothes and very inexpensive jewelry that I'd bought her. She unfolded a Hoodie and I could tell that she loved it (she always loved Hoodies when I bought them for her). Laying it on the table, she spread it out and, for a moment, Carm was Carm again, not a person with Dementia.

She looked at me and smiled again, then she kissed me on the cheek and I kissed her.

Only twenty minutes had passed. I asked Carm if she was doing okay and did she like the Nursing home. She shook her head, her auburn hair touching my face. She mouthed the word, "No" then, coughing, tried to say that simple word again. When she couldn't I turned to Carm's nurse.

"Nurse, I'm going outside for a moment."

You see, I had to. It was at that moment, when Carm couldn't say a simple "No" that I at last realised the extent of her illness. I went downstairs and outside. I started crying my eyes out. A woman who had just finished visiting her husband who was also a Resident saw me crying and, walking over, put her hand on my arm. She asked me why I was sobbing so hard. So I told her. And then I said, "I don't think I can go back in today. I'll come back tomorrow. You know, this is my fault, not Carm's."

That lovely woman was the first one to tell me, "Tom, stop beating yourself up. An illness is an illness and it wasn't your fault. My husband has dementia and for a long time I thought it was my fault, too. Then I thought it was his fault. Or someone else's fault. God's fault. Then I realized after I'd gone to counselling for a few sessions: it's no one's fault at all. These things happen to anyone; it doesn't matter if you're healthy or not; thin or fat; exercising or not. It often runs in families and that's no one's fault, is it? Are you okay now?"

Listening to her, I felt much better. For the very first time, I realised that Car's illness was not my fault. It was no one's fault. Then I remembered that Carm's mother had passed away due to Dementia. She had lived to be in her late-80's. That woman was right. It did run in Carm's family. And I also remembered that Dad had passed away in part from Dementia. So that illness ran in my family too.

And that's the lesson I started to learn. As I wrote at the top of this chapter, I still beat myself up. Tomorrow, I once again go to my wonderful friend, call her J again, and am having my 3rd counselling session with her. One of the things I'll talk to her about is how I still beat myself up in the morning and continue to think that it's all Tom's fault.

But it isn't.

Are you beating yourself up over something that you can't control? That's the question.

The answer is simple: as easy as saying "No."

The ANSWER is: "NO! I will NOT beat myself up right now. I'll do that tomorrow and I'll try not to do it again.

In another chapter I'll tell you how I did get to see Carm for a second time. That time, I saw her for a whole 5 seconds. The Director of Nursing saw me, told me I was not welcome, and had phoned the local Garda, our Police Force, to arrest me.

Looking back on it and what she tried to do to me, I have to laugh like hell! She could NEVER have me arrested! Why? I did nothing but ask to see Carmel Murray again and take her two bags of presents for her 60th birthday. But that's in another chapter.

That simple lesson the woman standing outside the Trim Nursing Home taught me I now give to you.

It is one of the most important Guidelines I've ever learned. Today, and I try to do this every day too, I tell myself:

"TOM, STOP BEATING YOURSELF UP FOR WHAT WAS NEVER YOUR FAULT."

I try, anyway.

Guideline Number 8

Be Kind to Yourself

> Guideline Number 8
>
> <u>Guilt is like Rust.</u> It eats you up and leaves only a husk of your former self. If you think you need help coping, go out and get it!

Guilt is like rust. I'm going to say that again: GUILT IS LIKE RUST. If you feel guilty about actions you've taken, you're no longer effective. In my case, extreme guilt was caused by the following: I fully believed that I was somehow responsible for Carm's Dementia (wrong, Tom). I believed that, when I couldn't get any lawyer to help me or when they were too busy it was my fault (wrong). I came to believe that because I could not see Carm, and had no access to her, it was because I'd become a bad man (wrong again). I came to believe that because many of my friends near where I now lived no longer wanted anything to do with me, it was because (place horrible swear word here - something like "Tom really did lock Carmel Murray in his shed and beat her senseless! The b***tard!!!!") (WRONG, WRONG, WRONG, ALL OF YOU!)

Guilt truly is like rust. Guilt can eat you alive. The Guilt that I had resulted in an inability to get sleep; I isolated myself from friends and family for months, I had no appetite or motivation to do much of anything; I stopped exercising, visiting friends or relatives, taking phone calls, checking the mail and otherwise stopped living. Those months were the most miserable of my life.

To give you a few examples of what happened to me when Carm left my life (which was NOT my fault nor was it hers. Even now, when I met some people who have accused me of being cruel to her, I'll tell them: "Sorry, but you're wrong! Go away and get out of my life." Which is what I still do occasionally. Of course, things still happen to me which are definitely unjust. But that's life and I try to keep a smile on my face despite the very large obstacles that appear. Some examples include:

- Taxes and the Stress of Them: As noted elsewhere, I am a tax resident in both Ireland and the United States, as is Carm. Each year since I came to Ireland, I file BOTH sets of taxes and pay those governments what is due. Recently, my tax accountant in the US filed my 2022 tax returns. I owed quite a bit of money to the IRS because I'd sold some assets in the US and had to pay capital gains tax. I sent a cheque to the US Department of the Treasury – and they never bothered to cash it. They lost the U.S. Check! So I sent another one. They lost that too! Finally, I sent a check to my Tax accountant (who is based in Florida) and he sent it to them. They took that check from him and now, those scums in the IRS, want me to pay even more! Like over $5,000 for no reason at all! Hell no, I'm not going to pay it. I don't owe it! So – this morning I sent my tax accountant yet another email asking him to take care of the IRS yet again! (When, and if, you get a professional lawyer or other professional to help you, try to relax. I always take comfort in knowing that I can place my problems on their knowledgeable shoulders and do my best to forget about it)

- So-called Friends: when everything hits the fan in your life you (and me) of course turn to close friends first. In hindsight, what amazes me is that the Close Friends that I counted on the most turned their backs on me. One group and one individual come to mind though there were many, many others.

- The Group – for many years I sang with a local Church choir. I made so many friends in that choir and many of them became close friends. I sang Baritone and, when I was finally ready to sing and our Church Services (I had to learn the music first, particularly the harmonies) I enjoyed it more than almost any activity I'd done at that point in my life. Carm always came along to Services. She'd sit at the back of our Church and from where I was sitting, I could see her smile and wave at me. A few years after I started singing, our Choir Director retired. She asked ME to 'take her baton" as it's often called so I became the Choir Director. To be honest, I worked my tail off. I learned all the music that the choir director taught us then started adding even more music, some of it rather complicated. The Choir LOVED not only the Music but also my Directing (and I told them when I picked up the Baton, "Friends, I've never directed before so have patience with me. And they did). As the months went on, that small choir was transformed into a LARGE CHOIR. We had over 40 people singing for Christmas Services. And they were FANTASTIC. They were so good that I told them I was going to soon enter them into County and National Choir Competitions. They were so surprised they started Applauding! I have so many pictures of Carm and I attending Services and how much Joy it gave both of us.

- Then things went horribly wrong. Carm was stolen, Covid struck (forcing us to close all Services) and I had that terrible Heart Attack. I contacted all of the Choir Members and told them that I'd be back as the Director when I fully recovered.

- Now, do you know what happened? These weren't good

friends. These choir members were FANTASTIC friends. I helped all of them over the years that I was singing and directing with them and they often helped me and Carm. Carm and I even had them over to our home to sing and practice on many, many weekends usually right before Easter and Christmas Singing Season. And yes, I have PICTURES, so many of them, that prove how close we all were. We were a FAMILY. At least I thought we were.

- When Carm was stolen from me, I told a number of very close members of this Loving Group what had happened. And you know what? Except for a handful of members, NO ONE phoned me or came to visit me even though they knew how much I was suffering. And when I had my heart attack? No one bothered visiting me when I came back home. A few people called, which was wonderful. I became so angry and guilt-ridden. I thought it was MY fault. Here, I'd like to point out that even now this is happening. Without Carm at my side, no one ever asks me up to their homes anymore (as Carm and I did together many times). No one calls to our home. Rarely does anyone phone to ask how Carm and I are doing. Not one member of the above Group. And except for two close male friends that I have in my Village (thank God for both of them) I would be isolated again. Not a way to live. Thinking about it, here's what I think is happening. When I was with Carm, we were considered to be a married couple. But now that I'm alone, I'm perceived as a threat to any couple that's dating, married or engaged. It's ridiculous but a reality. Both single males and females can be considered as threats to other close couples. The good thing? I answered my own question: Tom is not a threat to anyone! So the guilt is now gone.

- The second example concerns a person who shall remain nameless. Let's call them 'G'. It's a long story and I won't go into it again, but my phone was hacked – as was my laptop – any number of times. My bank then, a local Irish bank, froze all of my cash. I did not have access to the assets that I had in the States and so I was absolutely broke. I couldn't pay my mortgage, my electricity bills, buy diesel for the Pickup. I survived with a small amount that I had in a local Savings Account right across the street – about $70 – and some change that I found. Too, when I needed cash the most to survive another day or week, I found some neatly folded Euro Notes in Carm's trousers and coat pockets. It was as if she was helping me and I still believe that.

- But almost penniless, I went to G (who had many, many assets then) and asked if I could borrow €250. He knew what I had in the bank accounts that were frozen and all about the hacking. I pleaded with them. I begged them. And their answer despite having a fortune tucked away in all sorts of assets? "Tom, I'm sorry but the answer has to be 'No'. Never a borrower or a lender be. That's what my parents told me."

- I'd known this person for many, many years. I would lend him cash now and then when he was short. NO? To me? A close friend? What I've learned from all of the above is this: Those you THINK are your close friends are usually NOT your close friends. You'll only know when times become very, very difficult and you reach out to all of them for support. Those that take the time and go to the trouble to help you ARE YOUR REAL CLOSE FRIENDS. Such is life; such is reality.

- The problems above were caused by my vulnerability after Carm was stolen. Her absence left a whole in my heart that's as wide as the Universe. My vulnerability encouraged many people of both sexes to contact me via Social Media. Usually, they don't want friendship. They want cash. A number of times, just after Carm left my life and when I was at my lowest, I came very close to being sucked in by these many ruses and fake people.

- The Lesson here is THIS: DO NOT SUCCUMB TO YOUR LONELINESS AND VULNERABILITY. That too is like Rust. It can also eat you alive and ruin you financially if you fall for one of these perpetrators.

- Every week I read in the news of someone – a lonely man or women – who falls for one of these scumbags. The Scumbag usually says that they're 'So in Love with xxxx. I know you'll help me. I'm a zillionaire as you know but am sort of stuck for a few bucks right now. Would you mind sending me $xxx?" That, of course, is only the start of it. Many of these Victims send all the cash that they have to the Scumbag. All of their life savings. And they are financially ruined for the rest of their lives. As you all know, older people are usually the prey of this Thieves and Liars. But the Scumbags have zero ethics. All they care about is CASH not human beings.

- So if you're lonely, please be very, very careful. Pick one person to really trust. Share your soul with them and tell them what you need to share. It's almost like the Golden Rule. "Treat others as you want to be treated" turns into, at least for me, "Share with those that you trust what you need to share, and let those that trust you share with you."

- By doing that a few times a week, you're loneliness will disappear. You'll be less vulnerable and much less likely to make any mistake at all.

Guideline Number 9

Keep Active & Enjoy Life

> Guideline Number 9
> ... With a Strong Focus on your Objectives, Discipline and a strong work ethic. Enjoying life with many activities will help you pass the time until you / I can see (insert name here) Carm my Missing Partner / Wife / Life

As I know you understand, gaining access to Carmel Murray has been my single focus for a long, long time. In fact, ever since I discovered quite by accident that I'd been Denied Access to my wonderful woman possibly for the rest of my life. And yes, it IS still very depressing.

To start this chapter, let me describe how I first truly realised that I could not see Carmel whenever I wanted to - unlike most relatives and friends who want to visit their loved ones in any Nursing Home across the world.

Three months had passed since my last visit to see Carm. In the meantime, seven hours south of her in our home, I applied myself to making sure that we had enough money that when she came home I could take care of her. For that reason, I continued writing novels and screenplays one after another. I still had great trouble sleeping at night due to her continuing absence. With nothing else to do, I would work at least 10 hours a day, 7 days a week. I churned out Novels and screenplays, one after another, until my head spun. But during that time, I learned that my first Novel written for the Adult Market, had gone to Number 1 Globally. That damned Novel, which my Carm had helped me to edit and write, took off like wildfire all over the world. That success gave me renewed confidence in myself and kindled a new hope that Carm would come home soon.

"That novel, Dolphin Song, is a story of miracles. In many, many ways, it's about Carm and me and our little dog Jack. That plot has many differences to our lives, of course, but if a wife and her child can be transformed magically into Dolphins to join their long-lost Husband, then why can't Carm rejoin me, her 'missing' husband?" (You can see all of our Novels, non-fiction books, books for Children and Young Adults, memoirs and updates on our Feature Film Productions by going to www.storylinesent.com. Rightfully, Carm should be listed as a Co-Managing Director and Co-CEO but she's not here to sign the paperwork).

And rejoin her I would, at almost any cost. At this point, I'd hired a good solicitor to help me get access to Carm. Together, the solicitor and me hired a great Barrister. At a meeting where we were all present (except Carm) the Barrister said: "Tom, of course you'll have access to her. You're her Common Law Husband. Too, we'll soon be in Discovery regarding this new case and when that happens - a few weeks from now - you have every right in the world to see Carmel Murray."

I was absolutely thrilled - at least at that point. Right after that important meeting, I had to fly to London to attend the London Book Fair. My hope was to land a Literary Agent and perhaps sign a Global Deal for the Publication of the Novel Dolphin Song and attract finance to that Title's Feature Film. I went and worked hard for the five days I was there. When I came back to Ireland - and landed in Dublin Airport - my first thought was of Carm.

"Dammit, I missed her birthday again!" I thought as I drove down the M50 and back to Trim. "Her birthday, the 20th of May, was a few days ago. It's the 24th of May now so I'm not that late."

I stopped in Blanchardstown Shopping Centre (a few hours later I came to regret that decision) and bought Carmel two bags of clothing and jewelry at TK Max. Driving back up the M3, I found that I was so happy to be home and knew that I'd see Carm in about 20 minutes, depending on traffic.

Turning into the Parking Lot at that Trim Nursing Home, I looked at my watch and saw that it was only 1130 AM. The House Rules of most Nursing Homes are that when the Residents are having a meal, no one can visit. This way they can concentrate on eating which, for some, is quite hard to do. Walking into Reception with my two bags, I suddenly had a great foreboding. This is what my head told me:

"Tom, the last time you were here you were welcomed by every nurse and doctor you met. And Carm was Great and you both enjoyed your visit. But now things are very different. Whenever you phone the Nursing Home receptionists, they tell you that Carm can't talk to you and will not give you a status on her health."

In short, and for no real reason at all, I felt that this time I wouldn't be welcome to see my dear Pookey. At first, I realised I was wrong. When I went up to reception, I told them, "Hi, I'm Tom Richards, Carmel Murrays Partner. I have these two bags full of gifts for her birthday. I'm sure she's busy so I'll just leave them with you."

I placed the bags on the Reception desk and was turning to leave when the Receptionist looked up and smiled. "Mister Richards, please sign in." When I signed the visitor registration form, feeling rather uncomfortable again for no reason, she handed me a small slip of paper with a New Four Digit Number on it. "Tom, keep this with you and show it to any nurse you see. That's the code for the Security Door. The number," she used a pen to point to every digit, "If One-Four-Zero-One".

I took the piece of paper and put it in my back pocket. Taking the elevator upstairs (this time only one floor above reception) my heart beat faster and I felt a goofy grin spread across my lips). The elevator door opened and I stepped out. Meeting a nurse that I'd met the last time I visited, I held out a hand and she shook it, not letting my hand go. "Tom, you're so welcome back! Carm's waiting for you in the Day Room." She walked me up to the double doors, and looking inside, I could see Carm sitting in a large chair pushed against the far window talking to a woman on her right-hand side. I held up my hand and waved at her and, smiling at me, she waved back for a few seconds.

Then the lovely Day Nurse walked toward me. "Tom, I'm sorry but we're having lunch in only a few minutes. Can you come back here in an hour?"

"Sure I can. I'll go downstairs and wait in our Pickup Truck. I'll be back here in an hour." I lifted the two bags of gifts. "Nurse, these are presents for Carm's birthday. Can you give them to her?"

"Wait until you come back and then you can give them to her yourself."

I walked back the way I had come. On the way to the elevator I was met by two other Nurses. I had met both of them before.

"Mister Richards! What are you doing here! You've been barred from seeing Ms Murray."

I was staggered. Me? Barred from seeing Carm? "No I'm not. I was given the Code. See?" I showed them the small slip of paper and the tall Nurse frowned.

"You should NOT have been given that code. We must now escort you out of the Nursing Home."

As the three of us descended to the ground level, I was met by only silence when I asked any question. When the door opened, I once again asked a question. "Please, can I give you my side of the story?"

The tall nurse nodded and led me into the Nurses small office. As I explained why I was there and how I had been given that code, I could see their faces soften. I caught the glint of a tear in both of their eyes as the smaller Nurse reached for a tissue.

"Nurses, I'm here for one reason. To give Carm her birthday presents. I'm late for her 61st Birthday, don't you see? That's why I'm here."

"Tom we're all sorry," the tall Nurse said. "That's the law right now. You're not permitted to see her again."

I left the two bags with those very kind Nurses who were fully sympathetic to my plight. Turning to walk back through the door, I saw a woman I recognised marching down the hall toward me.

"Thomas Richards," the Director of Nursing cried. "What are you doing here? I'm having you arrested! I've called the Gards and they should be here any minute."

I looked at her and laughed. "Director I'm not causing a scene. My voice isn't as loud as yours. All I'm doing is leaving some presents for Carm and then I'm leaving."

Her eyes looked like storm clouds. "Get out of here right now! Never come back."

I tried to shake her hand but she refused. She turned on her heal and marched into the Nurses Office. As she shut the door on me, I could hear her say, "Never let that man in here again!" One of the Nurses replied, "But he's a nice man. Why?"

I sat the Pickup Truck and waited for the Gards to show up. Now here's the thing. Many Gards in the local Trim Garda Station are personal friends of mine. Many know Carm because she's lived in Trim for most of her life. When the Garda Police Car didn't show up, I laughed hard and made a great decision.

"What I'm going to do is report that Director of Nursing to the Gards for theft, refusing access to a legal partner, criminal intent because she threatened me physically (which that strange woman did), psychological damage and anything else I can think of."

The Garda Station is only a five-minute drive from the Nursing Home. When I arrived it was 1210 PM local time. The Garda on duty was a great fellow. He sat and I dictated my complaint for 45 minutes, maybe a bit longer. When we were finished, he looked at his watch. "Tom, go get some lunch while I punch your testimony into our Garda Computer System. Come back and I'll print it out. I'll sign it and you sign it and that's all you have to do."

Long story short, I did exactly what that Garda suggested. I had a quick bite to eat then came back to the Station and signed the document on all of it' pages. When we were finished I shook the young man's hand.

"Tom, what that Director of Nursing has done to you is ridiculous!" he said, laughing into his hand. "You have every right to visit your legal partner. If you don't have legal representation, I can recommend a few good firms in Trim."

He wrote down a list of recommended law firms, gave them to me, and when I came home I phoned a few. All of them said they couldn't take the case, though I would in all probability win and be able to visit Carm, but they were representing Residents in that Nursing Home.

Since coming home without Carm (the above 5 second visit happened about just over 2 years ago) I've kept incredibly active. This lets me at least try to put the issues and problems that Carm and I have out of my mind. So what do I do to stay active? Everyone has their own list of things they love or like to do which helps them to decrease stress. Here's my list (some of these activities are suggested by my Doctor and Heart Surgeon):

- Sailing (relieves stress and helps me concentrate only on sailing the boat)

- Weight lifting (I use two 5 KG weights, one in each hand. Usually, I'll sit in a chair and work out for between 10 and 20 minutes most days of the week. Sometimes I'm so tired physically I can't work out at all. Which is a healthy way to look at exercise

- Yoga – I stretch using Yoga positions every day. On days when I'm not lifting weights, I practice Yoga for somewhere between 15 and 30 minutes. I start by getting into a Yoga Position, Siddhasana, and completely relax. I'll think of nothing except my 3rd eye at my forehead and all of the chakras. I Practice a kind of Yoga called Kundalini. This means that I breath through my nose and mouth which helps me to release most of the stress in my body. I practice a combination of standard Yoga with a bit of Buddhism. This makes me totally relax. (In a chapter below, I'll quickly run through the various weight lifting positions that I do most days of the week as well as certain Yoga Positions. Together with the low-fat diet I'm on, I've managed to lose 10lbs over the past 6 months)

- Golf – keeps me very, very fit! The course that I play on (I'm a member of the Berehaven Golf Club) is a links course. Right on the sea, and with a few hills that make golfers walk up at a forty-degree angle, at first that course was impossible for me to play! Golf is the most frustrating, wonderful game I've ever tried. I'm terrible at it but when I'm playing and trying to hit that white ball with all of my might (that darned ball never goes where I want it to go) I'm thinking of nothing but the club that I'm using, the ball, the tee, how hard to hit the ball, and the pin – what I'm trying to aim at. I love this sport. I'll never be much good at it but it's a great pastime.

- Gardening – I love to garden in the backyard of our home. I've been planting vegetables ever since Carm and I moved in. Usually Potatoes, Rhubarb, Strawberries, Raspberries, Blueberries, beans and a great deal of flowers. I've also planted two apple trees. Gardening helps me to remember how Carm enjoyed our garden as much as I did.

- Flying – flying a light plane is very, very expensive in Ireland so this is an occasional 'hobby'. But just like sailing, when I'm flying I forget everything that's bothering me and only concentrate on flying the aircraft.

- Snorkelling – the Atlantic Ocean is very, very cold so I own a very thick wetsuite as well as a facemask, snorkel, small knife for scraping mussels off the nearby rocks, weights and fins. When Carm was here we'd go down to the local beach many times during the summer. I must admit though I love this sport, I don't go as often as I should. Snorkelling is great exercise and the salt water makes me feel good. I'm planning on bringing all of this equipment to the new sailboat soon. Late this summer, I hope to dive from the sailboat and snorkel in Bantry Bay. Now wouldn't that be lovely!

I have other pastimes that I work on occasionally: building small plastic model aircraft and playing the piano are just two. Piano playing is fun but really hard for me. When Carm was here and I was the director of the choir, I learned every single hymn that we sung, as well as some classical music, almost by heart. One piece of music, a work by Chopin, was so difficult that Carm (who was sitting in the next room and could see me through the open doors) would Applaud when I finally got at least half of it right. I don't play as often now. There's no one to play for except my lovely puppy. Though she loves me playing, it's not the same at all. Too, I enjoy walking my little Bluebell. She's been at my side since Carm was stolen from me. That little puppy is, I think, a gift from God or from Carm or maybe both. Pets certainly help me to feel less lonely.

I very much hope that anyone who is in the same position as I am has a pastime or two and perhaps exercises if you need to. I find that all of the above help me to pass the day alone and (usually) wake up in the morning feeling good and emotionally strong.

I've said this before: make certain that you get enough sleep every night. Eat at least something every day. Something that you enjoy; that's nutritious. If you think you need to go on a diet or want to exercise like I do, consult your doctor. He or she can come up with an appropriate plan for you.

The journey that I've been through for the past three years, my continuing demand to be able to access my loving legal partner, does seem never ending at times. That's the reason why I do my best to keep fit: when I someday do realise what at times seems like an impossible dream, I want Carm to be able to recognise the Tom that still lives in our Home.

Guideline Number 10

Keep Active & Enjoy Life!!!

> Guideline Number 10
> We are Entitled to a Future of Happiness, Joy and contentment – don't forget your own needs. My good friends and family members all say that I need to get out there to do what Carm and I used to do together.

Every now and then, usually after a therapy or counselling session, I can emotionally 'crash' like I did this morning. It makes no real sense! I had wonderful dreams about Carm last night. In one of them, we were sitting at the TV watching a Feature Film. Carm and I were eating Tacos again (that was one of our favourite meals). We were half-way through the Film when Carm asked me, "Pook, can I have another one? I'll put the Film on pause and then I can help you make four more - two each for both of us." We both got up and made the Tacos than sat down, watched the film and kept eating.

Yet when I woke up, it left me with nothing but a headache. Once again I suffered an emotional 'hangover' after a wonderful dream. I felt better after I had a shower and fed the two pets. Then I started working and now feel much better for sharing it with you.

I've resolved that I will never, ever be able to let go of Carmel, much less replace her. When Carm first disappeared from the village and we all thought that she was never come back (at that point I really did think that my Carm was dead) a good-hearted woman suggest that I date again. I've never, ever been good at dating. Carm and I didn't date. We really did fall in love at first sight. But, having thought about what the woman suggested, I tried online dating a few times and hated it. No one I saw on those dating sights attracted me and many of them were fake women (often gangs trying to rip me off). Yet, I don't want to live on my own anymore, either.

A number of years ago, Carm and I were sitting at our dining room table. We both knew it was time to plan for the future. Carm was somewhat worried about me in that, as I've written, I'm 8 years older than her. I wasn't worried about Carm, not really. And as for me? Like most couples I thought we'd both live forever. But after discussing the future, she said, "Tom, what happens if something happens to you? Let's say you suddenly drown or go down in an airplane. What do you want me to do?"

I remember smiling and shrugging my shoulders. "Sweetie, all I want you to do is to enjoy your life. Be happy. If you're lonely, find someone that you like. Go dancing and go out for meals like you and I always do. Laugh and listen to music. Be happy! And if you want to get married like we plan to, and find a man that you love, then marry him."

"Marry someone else?" she asked, her face blank. "But I love you and no one else."

At that point, I took her warm hand. "I know you do and you're the only person in my life. To me it seems we've been together since the beginning of time."

She smiled at that then got up and gave me a kiss. "You're a very good man, Tom. The best man on the planet."

Thinking back on that brief discussion I also remember that after she kissed me she stood over my chair, her hair falling onto my head, and massaged my shoulders and temples for a moment. I looked up at her.

"Carm, if something should happen to you - not that it's going to - what do you want me to do?"

"Exactly what you told me, Tom. Be happy. Marry someone if you can find that special person."

That memory isn't as fresh as I'd like it to be. Yet I remember every word of what we said to each other. This time I have no answer but I do have the Question:

"What should Tom do for the rest of his life?" Possible answers: Stay single and get over my loneliness. Do not isolate myself. Take one day at a time, one moment at a time. Breathe. Be at peace. Live and love my family.

Or: "Date a little if you can find someone that reminds Tom of Carm. Go out for dinner. Dance a bit. Laugh a bit. Try to enjoy my life."

Or: "If I can find someone that reminds me a little bit of Carm with the same ethics, courage and determination; if I learn to like that woman; if I fall in love and if she learns to love me, maybe just maybe we can get married." Or not.

I don't know what the future holds for me. My magic ball stopped working an age ago. So what would you do if you find yourself in the same position as me? Isolate yourself? Try to get through each day though the memories of your loving partner hurt like a knife stabbing your heart every day? Take life as it comes and just wait around your home? Stop even trying. "To hell with life and happiness," we all might say.

But none of the above are really good enough! Life is a real gift. I know now I have only one life and, because I'm 68, I'm in the last third of what God has given to me. All I want, as I've written before, is a little bit of happiness and some contentment. Yes, I'd love to have a Companion: someone that makes me laugh, that will go dancing with me, that will halt my loneliness in its tracks. But who?? Where are you, special woman? Where?

Maybe nowhere. Maybe that woman doesn't exist. Or maybe she does exist and right now is getting ready for her lunch in that far off Day Room I visited one time. Maybe her name is Carm or Charm or Carly. I don't know. Maybe it doesn't matter.

Maybe happiness for me is to be found only in my dreams which isn't terrific but sometimes it suits me fine. Or maybe not.

Do I seem confused? Damned right I'm confused. And I know that many of you who read this are also confused. The answer to the Question: Keep Active and Enjoy Life!!! is a hard one to answer. Each of us has a slightly different definition of Happiness. To some it means absolute Joy! To others it means Awesome! To yet others Happiness means financial success and the flexibility to stop worrying about the future.

To me, right now as I finish this chapter, it simply means this: My happiness depends on the People that I'm truly close to. It is defined as my way of coping and of what I do every day. It is a sad sort of happiness. A terribly lonely brand of happiness. Yet, I am entitled to this type of happiness, too.

Someday, God willing, Carm will come home again. On that day I will be TRULY HAPPY! And if she doesn't come home, then I'll have to find another definition of Happiness. A good woman. A wonderful Life. A bit of Joy. And a God-Given way of Living that will finally give the rest of my Life a great deal of Peace.

Guideline Number 11

Learn to Share with Close Friends

> Guideline Number 11
> When you do, when you find those people who you can trust to share a secret or two, you'll feel much better.

I've decided that some people are very, very strange. Not odd. Strange. You'll be talking in your local bar and the bartender will be listening. He'll look at you and say, "Why are you expressing that opinion in here? Is that the only reason you come in here, to talk with your friends? Stop talking, watch the television and buy another beer or get out of here and don't come back!"

Odd and strange, no? Yes! People can be selfish and rude. Some people don't listen. Some can be self-destructive and in the process harm you. People you trust can betray you all the time, particularly those who you thought were your good friends.

So who do you talk to if you just want to share something very private and don't want to go to a counsellor? Here's what I do and I hope it helps.

First, and just as I'm doing here, I write things down. What I'm feeling and thinking. Why I'm feeling the way I am. Right now I feel somewhat tired due to the fact that I woke up so abruptly this morning. I write and write about how I feel then what I might do today.

I'll reread that a few times and if I've forgotten something I add that. If something is way too private to share with someone I cross it out. Then I make a decision on who to share it with.

Finances. Problems and issues associated with Carm. Daily living: I have friends who sort of 'specialise' in these subjects. A great friend of mine who I trust with my life helps me with any financial decision that I have to make. To be honest, and due to the high stress levels I've endured and maybe it's because I'm getting older, I will NOT make a major financial decision without consulting this good man. Period. I recommend that you do the same. Find someone you TRUST with regard to your personal finances, be that a family member, a trusted tax accountant or other professional, or a person who has a background in finance. When Carm was here, she was my financial advisor. We'd discuss everything, every detail, before we made a financial decision together. But now? That's why I also have a few great financial advisors (who are also financial managers at large banking companies) who are also trusted friends. But I'll only discuss long-term strategies with them. After all, and unlike what some people think, my personal financial affairs are my business.

As for Carm: I've mentioned my trusted counsellor, J, above. Right now, she is the only person I talk to in detail about my life with my Partner. Yes, I talk to my children now and then. And yes, I talk to my two good male friends. But not in depth. They simply don't understand why I continue to feel the way I do. Some of my friends tell me, "Tom, it's been three years since she left. Maybe, just maybe, she left you because she wanted to lead her own life again." Not true! Of course it's not true. And as for my children: they have their own lives. The last thing I want to do is burden them with the intimate details that Carm and I experienced. Why do that when I can talk with J?

Daily Living is the easiest of these three. I can talk to almost anyone about most things: what I'm making for dinner. How the sailboat is and when will I go sailing again. What's on the news and why it matters. Politics. Exercise. Woodworking (another of my hobbies). This list also goes on and on. Talking about the small things, I find, really helps me lower my stress levels. It's the small things that make me feel a bit better. Sometimes much better. It's the small things in life that are normal! And I don't have a normal life anymore.

If you need to talk about your Absent Partner, maybe you need to talk to a professional. A third party that doesn't know either of you very well. As I think I mentioned above, I've had a number of counsellors over the years. J really is special. She listens and listens to me talk (it's more like a conversation). She'll then comment about what I say and sometimes, if it's relevant, give me some good advice which I always take. Try to find someone like that. J has really made a difference to my life.

As for the other topics in this chapter? That's up to you. Find people you trust before you share anything at all. Some people love to gossip. You might say to someone you know well: "Did you know that I had a scan for cancer?" A week later, you'll discover that someone, a close friend of the person you shared with, has told someone else, "Did you know that XXX died of cancer? Isn't that horrible! I told her years ago that she should quit smoking!"

What they don't know but you do is that a) you're still alive and b) you quit smoking over a year ago.

To sum up: be careful who you share with. Then, when you make your decisions, share everything that's relevant. When you do, you'll feel like you're in Safe Hands. Just like the old Allstate Farmers Insurance Ads that I saw at Illinois Wesleyan University: "You're in Good Hands with Allstate!" I wish it was that simple. A simple Ad taken out on TV telling everyone about Carmel Murray and what we've both gone through.

Guideline Number 12

Hope. A Profound Sometimes Gift

> Guideline Number 12
> Hope can be very elusive. But HOPE gives all of us strength to face the uncertainty that we all go through sometimes for a lifetime.

Hope. I'm going to scream that single word now and I hope you'll join me. HOPE! HOOOOPPPE! HOOOPPPPPEEEEEE!

There. I feel better and I hope you do too. Hope, at least for me, really has been elusive. Over the past three years, I feel like I've been playing tennis. The ball goes back and forth so much that my neck hurts. It's like being on a roller coaster. Up we go. Down we go. Sideways we go. But we are never let out of the car. That roller coaster ride seems endless.

When Carm first disappeared from the Village, and for many months after, I'd 'track' my progress of being able to see her again. I'd climb up the steps to our bedroom. Half way up I'd think about my day. "Okay, that's three steps up." I'd walk up three steps. "And six backward steps." I'd walk down the steps and find myself in our living room again.

Hope is sometimes impossible. Fortunately, I don't have to 'count up and back down the steps anymore'. Some time ago, I stopped counting. I'll be

Carm's sole Decisionmaker or at least get to see her sometimes rather soon. This year, perhaps. By my birthday in October? Perhaps but more unlikely with each passing day. Right now, it's the month of August. All the courts are closed in Ireland for this entire month. In some ways that's rather nice! It gives me a chance to pause. To take a break. To read and write. To write this to all of you. To think a bit. And to know that finally, I'm in safe hands. I have two great lawyers and two great barristers working on my Case to win Carm back. It won't be easy and all we can do is try our best. I keep saying my prayers. I keep eating. I keep working out to gain even more strength, courage, fortitude, persistence and energy. I keep my head down and work hard. That's daily living and, like you, how I try to earn my crust every day.

This final chapter is again a short one. In that Carm isn't home yet, it's not the end of my journey. Maybe ending this short book here is a good thing. Someday, I'll rewrite the ending to tell all of you what happened to Carm. What happened to me. How I've changed and who I've become. The old Tom? I don't think so. I can never become the old Tom Richards again. Life has hurt so much that it's changed the very fibre and soul of my being.

Hope. That's all I wish and pray for all of us. A little bit of Hope goes a long way to create a Little Bit of Happiness and Contentment.

God bless all of you. I hope your wishes come true as I hope Carm's wishes come true. And, well, I hope my wishes come true, too, someday. Maybe soon. Who knows.

Be well. If you want, email me. My email address is: tomrichards141@gmail.com. Looking forward to hearing from you and I dedicate this to all of you who are, or have, suffered like Carm and I have.

Tom Richards

15 August 2024

Eyeries, County Cork, Ireland

My Home and Carmel Murray's, Too.

–An Ending and a New Beginning, Too–

Appendix:

- Yoga – some Postures and positions. Remember, if something hurts STOP! If something works, CONTINUE!

Buddhist Chakras – a 'Chart'. I personally find that practicing Buddhism helps me terrifically! The Chakras pictured below are 'points of energy' in your body. Focus on THEM and not the Pain that's in you. Touch your body as it shows in the Chart, Breathe Out, and gain a sense of Long-Termed Peace.

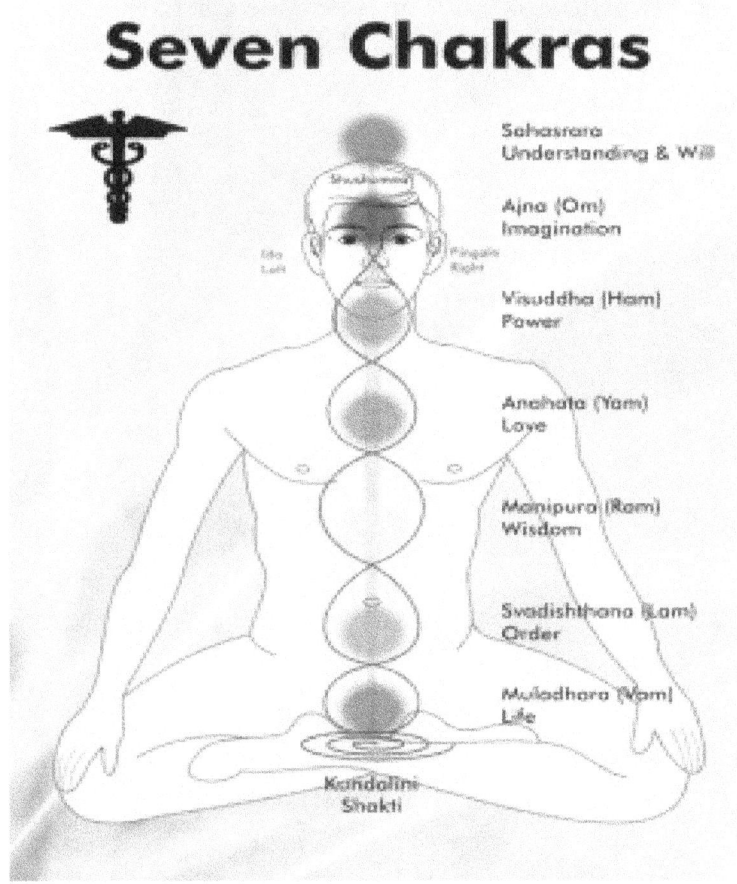

Weight Lifting – as I've written, I use relatively light 5KG weights. Do go to your local Doctor to ask him / her to help you plan your exercises and lose weight if, like me, you have to. IF SOMETHING HURTS STOP IMMEDIATELY! Don't hurt yourself. It's just not worth more pain! I include 2 simple exercises, below. I usually do 5 to 7 exercises, in 5 to 7 different positions, most of them on a chair. For more Chair Exercises, Google Chair Weight Lifting Exercises.

Acknowledgements

To all those very special people who contributed in any way to the writing of this book. As I say at the start, they are 'anonymous' for good reason.

To J, my counsellor and therapist. Much of what I've written was inspired by you.

To Simon and Frank. Thank you for being such good friends and allowing me to share with you what's been important in my life. To Liam G, my thanks for being there for me.

To all the people in this small Village of Eyeries who have supported me and cared for me. In particular: Francis, Claire and a host of others. To L P, my personal financial advisor. To my new Legal Team who is fighting to get Carm home to me: P L and C L. To my other team of wonderful lawyers who are fighting for me now: T O'R & C. To the many friends I have in the States including but not limited to Jackie H, Karisha S, Bill L, Willie A, Elle Rose, Ron R and his good wife F, Fred Schimmelman, and all of those who are living or have passed on.

To all the widows and widowers across the world who have lost their partners / husbands / wive / sons / loving friends / relatives to the Sea. I know you're pain because I'm now on your endless Voyage.

To the 'Ghosts' of my parents and Carm's parents: Mary, Bill, Josephine and Tommy. Wherever you are, keep doing it for all of our Happiness!

And finally, to Carmel Murray my loving wife and Pookey. You're here right now, standing at my side as I finish this. I'm convinced that, like J said, you're whispering in my ear, dictating what I should right. Thanks, Pook, for always being there.

Those who read this might ask, "But Carm isn't there! She's in a nursing home! Right?"

Carm and I both shout at the same time: "WRONG, WRONG, WROING AGAIN!"

Good luck to all I have NOT mentioned for very good and obvious reasons: I loved you like family but you all Betrayed Carm and Me.

And to all of you who still wonder about YOUR loving partner, know this: I pray for all of you every night before I go to bed. I hope you'll pray for Carm and me. Bless you all and a God-Given Great Amen.

Other Novels and Books written by Tom Richards

- Fiction for Adults
- Dolphin Song *
- Always Come Home *
- Lost Lovers *
- Happiness and Heartbreak
- UnBaptized **
- Annie's Joy **
- Remembrances **
- The Dazzling Universe of Helen Fox
- The Madness of Chief Inspector Mary Sweet
- Book 2 of the Mary Sweet Detective Series – The Scottish Caper
- Fiction for Young Adults & Children
- Hotfoot
- Hotfoot 2: Lucky's Revenge
- The Lost Scrolls of Newgrange
- The Den Adventure
- Sue the Two-Headed 'Roo and You

Jungle Juice Jim (in progress) *

Non-fiction

A Survivor's Guide to Living in Ireland

How a Yank Survives in Southwest Ireland (for well over 40 Years)

* Denotes Feature Films or Television Series of these Novels

Soon in Production

** Denotes Novels in development

www.ingramcontent.com/pod-product-compliance
Lightning Source LLC
Chambersburg PA
CBHW050233120526
44590CB00016B/2073